Chester E. Swor

NEITHER DOWN NOR OUT

BROADMAN PRESS
Nashville, Tennessee

Dewey Decimal Classification: 248.8
Library of Congress catalog card number: 67-12175
Printed in the United States of America
3.5JY6713

DEDICATION

To all to whom life has brought what the world calls handicaps, with the hope that these pages will perform a ministry of renewed faith, heightened courage, and increased joy in the inevitable victory which can be had over any, every handicap. . . .

To wonderful doctors, nurses, and hospitals whose ministries have saved life, lengthened usefulness, and relighted candles of hope in hearts which might have given up in despair. . . .

To all who have "stood by" in love, patience, and priceless assistance to help those whose lives have been touched with infirmities which came to stay, standing in the background of those who have turned defeat into victory, but "standing tall" in the sight of God and in the hearts of those whom they have helped.

CONTENTS

How This Book Began

This drawing is designed to indicate that the handicapped people presented in the following chapters are "in flight to lives of top-flight usefulness."

The brush drawings opening this and following chapters are by artist Nellie Faye Parker whose arms are paralyzed.

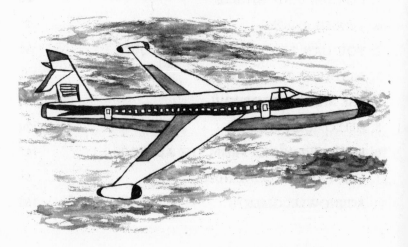

Neither Down Nor Out!

1

In the beautiful Crystal Room of a Dallas hotel a remarkable group met for a banquet and for the annual "Hurdle Awards" announcements. The Soroptimist Club of that city had asked clubs and individuals to submit names of people who had overcome very real handicaps to the point of achieving preparation and usefulness; and, from that list of nominees, a panel of judges had chosen a top-award winner and several nominees for honorable mention.

As the awardees were introduced, the nature of their individual handicaps was indicated, and a summary of their remarkable "hurdling" of these handicaps was given. That was an experience which I shall not only never forget: I shall never lose the thrill which the presentations brought! All of the honor winners had faced difficulties which would have crushed the spirit and killed the initiative of some people, but these heroic ones had been truly *neither down nor out.*

There was a twenty-three-year-old victim of cerebral palsy, who had chosen to transfer from a school for handicapped children to a public school, had dared to participate in the activities designed for completely well people, had achieved a bachelor of science degree with high honors, had earned a master's degree in rehabilitation counseling, and had returned to Dallas as a counselor in connection with psychological diagnosis and research concerning the various methods by which handicapped people can become more productive citizens.

Another awardee had been born without hands, but with mechanical hook hands had become inspiringly versatile. He had become quite a radio mechanic, he played three sports, he handled a paper route, and he planned to go to college for a major in electronics. Still another awardee had been stricken with polio while in the Army; and, at the peak of recovery, he could use only a badly impaired left hand. Even so, he entered university, received a degree and went into insurance—first over the telephone, then in his own office. He has not permitted his handicap to keep him from wide participation in community activities. In his chair he attends his civic club, P.T.A., Scout meetings, and his church, and he participates actively in official capacities in each.

One after the other, these magnificent heroes and heroines were presented to the acclaim of a large audience until, finally, the Hurdle Award winner was presented. She was a beautiful, charming, fascinating young woman who had suffered from athetoid cerebral palsy, a circumstance arising from damage to the motor area of the brain and causing a muscle tension which makes walking, talking, and use of the hands a tremendous difficulty. Challenged by the possibility of being able to overcome this three-way handicap, she had chosen public school, a speech therapy major in the university, and a speech therapy special education major for a master of arts degree! She had overcome fears of walking and appeared that night in high spike heels, and she had routed the fear of her hands by achieving excellence in painting. She was serving as principal of a school of special

Personal Enrichment 1968

Dorothy Fields June 1968
Rena Wolf July 1968
Ina Fifer Sept 1968

NEITHER DOWN NOR OUT

education and had just been accepted by a large university for work on a doctor of philosophy degree. Her speech of acceptance was a masterpiece of courage, poise, good humor, charm, and inspiration to others whom the world calls "handicapped."

I went from the banquet hall out into the crisp, cool night of that November experience with this feeling: whereas, it has been said of some handicapped people, "They are down, but not out," it can be said of the honorees of this memorable evening of accolades: "THESE ARE NEITHER DOWN NOR OUT!"

Several years have elapsed since that glorious evening; and, in those years, I have met personally or indirectly through correspondence a great concourse of heroic people of the sort who thrilled my heart in the Hurdle Awards Banquet. I have sat at their bedsides or chairsides; I have walked with them as, without fear, each has lighted a candle of confidence in his own heart that *no handicap, however seemingly impossible to overcome, is beyond the power of God and the courage of the individual to conquer.*

This book has been prepared as a tribute to the greatest conquerors of our time—those who have conquered self-pity, fear, discouragement, and defeat in their own hearts, and have marched forward to resourceful living despite their blinded eyes or deafened ears, despite their distorted bodies or shattered dreams or broken hearts, despite limitations of encroaching old age, despite even early failures and blemished lives. This book contains some of their stories, their struggles, their formulas for victory—their living proof that it is possible for a person with even the gravest handicap to be *neither down nor out!*

It is appropriate to begin this volume with a poetic salute

to all those who are achieving victory over handicaps with a title poem, a poem written by one who, throughout her life, has never walked, and who does not hear the sounds of our world, but who has demonstrated gloriously that handicaps can be God's doors to a very great usefulness to one's fellowman. Let me introduce you to Miss Jane Merchant of Knoxville, Tennessee. Now, hear her wonderful tribute.

FOR THE VICTORIOUS

Give glory to God
For the spirit of people who are born deformed
Or deaf or blind, who live glad lives of service;
For the spirit of people shattered in mid-career
By illness or accident, who begin again
And build good lives with the fragments that remain;
For all who make the best of the worst, transforming
Incredible disaster to unbelievable triumph.

Give glory to God
For people who are neither down nor out,
Who are up to life's most challenging demands
And in on the secret of victorious living,
Who are more than conquerors through Him Who loves us.

JANE MERCHANT

The Parade of the
2 Wouldn't Soldiers:
THEY WOULDN'T GIVE UP!

In this division of our book the reader is invited to imagine himself seated in a reviewing stand, observing an unusual parade, a parade consisting entirely of people whom the world calls handicapped. It is, indeed, a "Brigade of the Brave" and will pass by in good military fashion: battalions, companies, and platoons.

BATTALION ONE

Company A: Surprised, but Not Overwhelmed.

With the suddenness of a surprise attack from an enemy these heroic ones were touched by potential tragedy: *Mrs. Homer Null,* for instance. She and her family had gone to the mountains for the summer, the husband commuting to Houston, Texas, as his business required. They were unaware that a butane gas pipe had been damaged by landscape work, that a leak had occurred, and that the heavy gas had settled underneath the house. When someone struck a match to light a bathroom heater, a terrific explosion occurred: a six-year-old son was killed, a house guest suffered a shattered ankle, and Mrs. Null suffered the shattering of both of her legs.

The nearest hospital was many miles away, and so was an ambulance; however, Mrs. Null, with composure which

amazed everyone, remained conscious and gave directions for preventing unnecessary loss of blood. The damage to her limbs was so extensive, and the appearance of infection was so threatening, that amputation was decided upon as the only hope of saving her life. Prior to the operation, Mrs. Null, with spiritual power that thrilled and amazed, requested that prayer be made, and she led the prayer! Her pastor said this of her heroism and influence:

Doctors and nurses in the hospital say that the hospital will never be the same again because of her testimony and because of her spiritual influence. . . . I can bear testimony that she has been an inspiration to hundreds and hundreds of people. Without resentment, without bitterness or self-pity, she accepted the responsibility of wife and mother and accepted responsibility in her church, working in the Nursery department and making her influence count for Christ.

Mrs. Melva Platt enjoyed to the fullest her role as wife, mother of three splendid children, participant in church and civic activities in an Iowa town. What had begun as a happy and congenial drive with her husband and another couple ended suddenly with the car's overturning several times, leaving Mrs. Platt pinned beneath it, and destined to the role thereafter of a quadruplegic—paralyzed in both arms and legs. Tremendous faith and four years of determined effort made possible her returning to a semblance of normalcy in looking after her household and later to the beginning of a university curriculum to make possible her wider usefulness in educational services in the future.

All America gasped at the suddenness of the accident which retired world champion pole vaulter *Brian Sternberg* from athletic competition to possible permanent infirmity. He was busy in his regular practice on a trampoline as part of his preparation for pole vaulting skill and fell while performing a challenging double somersault and twist. "Probability of permanent paralysis is high," the terse report of the doctors announced.

The evidence of the real champion heart which he had came out immediately, however. The newspapers reported that Brian had said to his parents within seventy-two hours of the accident: "Watch the motion in my hand. I am working on it now. Watch my fingers. I'm sending impulses for them to move. I really believe I'm going to make it."

This champion of the athletic world has become in these years a champion of faith, courage, and victory in the world of the handicapped. A tremendous religious experience has been a part of his life since 1963; his testimonies in the Fellowship of Christian Athletes and its publications are profoundly moving; his handwritten note to Mrs. Kennedy

a year after his accident and her tragic loss represented a
victory greater than his record of breaking the world record
twice in polevaulting. His spirit has "vaulted" an immeasurably higher hurdle than his agile body ever did in the
preaccident days!

Just as suddenly, polio tapped *Miss Louise Luck* of Richmond, Virginia, on the shoulder and "pledged" her to the
sorority of neither-down-nor-out heroines. She was a teacher
in a junior high school when polio came; and, after three
years of treatment, including a sojourn in Warm Springs,
Georgia, she was able to walk with heavy leg braces and
two canes. Declining an offer to remain in Warm Springs as
a teacher, because she preferred to go back into the world of
the nonhandicapped, Miss Luck voiced this challenging
philosophy: "It's always been my aim to keep going regardless of what comes along. I've always told myself I won't let
anything get me down."[1]

"After three years and thousands of exercises later (eight
hours daily), Louise, in heavy steel braces, was walking
slowly and painfully," wrote a devoted friend.[2] It took the
better part of a morning or afternoon to walk to the end of a
short block and back. With courage and determination she
learned to drive a car again with the help of special equipment.

When she was offered a teaching position at Chandler
Junior High School, the doctor said it would be a blessing
for her; but it has proved, also, a blessing to thousands of
boys and girls, parents, teachers, principals, and others who
have come under the influence of her radiant Christian personality.

In her years of teaching and counseling in Chandler
Junior High, she was literally shackled to her chair and

desk, but the canes and legs with their heavy braces were carefully kept out of sight; and, in meeting her, one never knew from her face—alway lighted up with a warm smile—that she was handicapped in any way. Her complete selflessness, her love of people, her sympathetic understanding of the problems of life, her ready willingness to listen to the sorrows and trials and problems and joys and interests and pleasures of all who came her way endeared her to multiple thousands.

In her many years of teaching at Chandler Junior High, Miss Luck missed only a few days, and they were days of funerals for her devoted mother and brother. Heavy snows kept many of the students away, but not Miss Luck. Devoted students of Chandler met her at an entrance door each morning and assisted her to her counseling quarters. Her courage and determination in vacation times made possible her traveling by car throughout the United States, Canada, and Mexico, much of the driving being her own. The neither-down-nor-out spirit has carried through in her living arrangements. For most of her handicapped years she spurned a wheelchair, fearing that she might become dependent upon it; and she has done a full array of household chores with assistance of canes, braces, and a rolling table.

While Miss Luck was in her busiest years in Chandler High School, a discerning news reporter interviewed her and many of her devoted friends. The reporter summarized her magnificent spirit and that of the thousands of whom she is a bright and shining exemplar, people whose lives have been touched so suddenly by a come-to-stay handicap:

The children trust her completely. Many a girl bares problems of the heart she can't share at home. . . . Her callers at the school office often have included parents who come in to talk about themselves, not their children. And in many a case Miss Luck has been able to patch up a broken home when other agents have failed. . . . Strangers go out of her office not even knowing that she sits molded in her desk with heavy steel braces on each leg, and that she can rise with difficulty to only a half-erect position. She keeps two walking canes carefully concealed beside her chair. . . .

. . . She sits at her desk seven hours each day, radiating optimism over the most serious problems she is asked to counsel: the student who can't get along with his classmates or his teacher, the child whose parents are in bitter argument, the girl who has lost her true love, the parent who wants to know why his child is failing. All find a cheerful word and encouraging advice when they speak with Miss Luck.[3]

One of the students in Chandler Junior High declared, "She's the best friend I ever had," and many other former students around the world are saying the same thing.

In July of 1965, "school was out" for Miss Luck: retirement day had arrived, and many thousands of hearts in Richmond and elsewhere thanked heaven and Miss Luck for the rich legacy of radiance and unselfish living which had characterized her professional career. At this writing, cards, letters, telephone messages, and personal calls continue to reach her every week, serenading her happy heart with the sweet music of friendship and gratitude. But wait . . .

Don't conclude that this valiant woman has "taken to the rocking chair"! Shortly after her retirement, she flew to Hawaii for a tour of all the islands in our fiftieth state, amazing everyone with her courage, adjustability, and sheer joy in the arduous task of getting on and off planes eighteen times during the tour. When your author called her over the telephone in April of 1966, she had just returned from a busy round of calling upon former students and friends in Richmond. Indeed, Miss Luck is a magnificent example of the conquering philosophy which has helped her and so many other suddenly handicapped ones: *"I've always told myself I won't let anything get me down."* AND SHE AND THEY HAVEN'T!

Company B: Rolling Thrones

In this section of our parade of the handicapped-but-victorious ones we are overwhelmed with admiration as we observe that every participant is moving happily along in his or her wheelchair! Some have good use of their arms and can propel themselves with agility in their chairs; others, stricken in arms also, depend upon friends to assist them. There goes *Mrs. Polly Spangler* of California, stricken by both bulbar and spinal paralytic polio in 1954, but named in a recent year as "March of Dimes Mother of the Year." Her husband devised the battery-powered chair in which she rides triumphantly; and, while in the world of home, she carries on wonderfully and winsomely as a homemaker.

Waving at friends who watch the parade and who spot a Mississippi girl in the wheelchair section is *Jeannette Barksdale*, polio handicapped. She symbolizes the neither-down-nor-out spirit of many who have gone through college as "wheelchair students." The beribboned document which she is clutching so fondly in one hand is her diploma from the Mississippi State College for Women.

Also in this joyous section of our parade is *Paul Hibbard* of South Carolina, unable to use either hands or feet. The only part of his body which he can move without assistance is his head—but what a head!

Frank Logan, dean of students at Wofford College, says:

In my 47 years of living and 20 years of working with college students, this is by far and large the single most outstanding example of courage and bravery under almost overwhelming odds that I have ever known. This young gentleman, after his attack of polio, was left for functional purposes only his head, and he has used it in a magnificent manner. His spirit was such an inspiration to us here at Wofford that I hated to see him leave, naturally rejoicing in his successes while a student here.

He earned everything he got here, nobody gave him anything, he never asked for any favors. His attendance record was outstanding, and I saw him many times being pushed across the campus covered by a piece of canvas on a rainy day when other students would not get out of bed to come to class. He did this in spite of the fact that it was most important for him not to get pneumonia or get a cold because of the manner in which he had to breathe.

His brilliant mind, his magnificent personality, his tremendous courage all remain fixed in my mind; and, whenever I become weary and depressed about the burdens which life seems to push in on all of us, the memory of Paul Hibbard and what an example he is setting for the rest of us brings me back to reality and gives me strength to continue my own work.

The diploma in his lap indicates his graduation from Wofford College with high honors, and that pin on his lapel is the universally respected Phi Beta Kappa key. That determined smile on his face indicates that he is not through with higher education, and more bulletins can be expected from him. *Bulletin number one* advises that Paul Hibbard is now in his third year of Law School. Stand by for later bulletins.

Gwin Shelton entered a car one day, well, happy, purposeful, and just a month away from high school graduation. She was removed from the wreckage of the car with injuries which crippled her for life, paralyzed from waist down, and destined for the wheelchair constituency, but definitely not "out of the running" for success and happiness. After five years of physical complications, courage, and training, she is now a successful secretary for a law firm. Notice how expertly she handles her chair? She and a great host of her "chair-fellows" handle *all* of their lives that expertly!

And there are so many others in this glorious "rolling thrones" section of the parade. . . . But, to conclude our survey of this section of the parade, let's hear the thrilling story of another of the "wheelchair champions," whose achievements typify the victories of the occupants of these "rolling thrones."

As *Byron McKee* ran through the rain across the campus of Oklahoma State University in 1938, the nerves in his back seemed to give way completely. From Oklahoma City to Rochester, Minnesota, and to clinics in between he was taken, followed by the prayers and good wishes of the students from his campus, on which he had risen to positions of unusual honor and influence. The verdict was final: he would never walk again; a wheelchair became his throne and home.

Byron became one of the ever-growing concourse of courageous people who, though physically "down" for a count, are most surely not "down" spiritually nor "out" of the running! Sustained by a victorious Christian faith, he began to adjust himself to his new circumstances immediately, to seek for money-earning tasks which he could do, and to carve out a career of Christian usefulness in church and community.

Workwise, Byron went to work in a filling station! Though his admiring townspeople were not surprised to see a wheelchair attendant, we can well imagine the consternation of the out-of-town customers at the facility and happiness of this "man on wheels." This experience did far more for him and others than bringing a bit of money into his pocket: it proved to his own believing heart and to friends all around that Byron *could* overcome the handicap of an invalid's chair and could do so with efficiency and joy.

Eventually Byron went into the chicken and egg business, and ran the concern with amazing agility. He propelled his chair on ramps between the nests and feeding trays; and, with arms and shoulders greatly strengthened by courage and exercise, he was able to do a wide variety of plain physical labor. When a tornado blew the chicken houses away in 1960, he reported with courage undiminished and humor high that "not a hen was lost."

Churchwise, Byron never permitted his being "chairborne" to deter him from attendance and participation. He became active immediately in his home church, led his family to active participation, taught Sunday School classes, led youth groups, and was chosen deacon. To pastor and congregation he has been a powerful and perennial inspiration.

And romance, too! A lovely young woman came into Byron's community to teach in the public schools. A friendship developed, grew into romance, and eventuated in marriage—to the delight and good wishes of the whole community. The McKees felt that God was particularly generous to them in making possible their adopting a precious little girl. Is it necessary to say that blissful happiness has come to the McKee household?

Though Byron McKee never dreamed that a perfectly well body would suddenly wither into infirmity, he came to that memorable day on the Stillwater campus in 1938 prepared with a Christian faith so strong that he believed even then that "all things work together for good to them that love God,

to them who are the called according to his purpose," and
that "in all these things we are more than conquerors through
him that loved us" (Rom. 8:28, 37). He *knows* now from the
crucible of experience what his heart *believed* then through
the principle of faith.

Company C: Paralyzed, but Productive.

In the long ago, the word *paralysis* carried with it the
sound of doom and the implication that the paralyzed person
would exist as an object of pity and as a continuing responsibility to family and friends. How wonderfully that picture
has changed! The late President Roosevelt probably did
more than anyone else in the history of our nation to dispel
through his example the thought that paralyzed people
should not tackle the hardest jobs or strive for the highest
positions. In recent years the company of paralyzed-but-
productive citizens has been an inspiring section in the
parade of the "Wouldn't Soldiers." Let's meet some representatives of this remarkable group.

Texan *Florrie Conway* was only two years of age when
polio called upon her. Her life was spared, but she was
badly crippled. Although some doors of "growing up"
activities were shut to her, the bright lights of courage and
hope kept her from despair—even when she lost her father
just prior to her emergence into teen years.

Patience, perseverance, hard work, and dedication in
Florrie Conway's life paid rich dividends. She graduated
from high school and university, accepting an interlude of
gratifying church staff positions thereafter. Then, with the
dream of wider usefulness to impel her, she returned to the
largest university in the Southwest for a master of library

science degree. For more than a decade she has headed the library staff of Wayland College in Plainview, Texas, dispensing through word and example the confident assurance that paralysis and productivity are *not* strange partners!

Now, meet *Larry Allison*. He is typical of the throng of young men who have "kept rendezvous" with polio, who have wrestled through months and years to retrieve as much physical agility as possible, and who have achieved victory over discouragement and despair.

Larry's experience with polio began when he was ten years of age and at the height of his love for neighborhood football. In fact, he was in the midst of an exciting game with his pals when a severe headache necessitated his going home and to a doctor. The log of events thereafter will be familiar to thousands of other polio "alumni" and their families: hospitalization (a whole year before his first visit home), hot packs, exercises interminable, hope kindled, hope diminished, hope renewed, braces, crutches, slow progress, thirteen operations, and a struggle all the while to keep from settling for less than God's best use of his life in vocation.

Thanks to continuing instruction in school subjects in hospitals and to his schoolteacher mother, Larry was able to return to school in the same grade in which he would have been without the polio interruption. In high school and college years he faced and conquered natural shyness and self-consciousness, accentuated by his handicap. He disciplined himself to participation in a widening scope of school and church activities, asking no special consideration because of his handicap. With widening participation came deepening confidence—even the confidence that professional school was not beyond his capacity to handle.

Graduating from college, he attended seminary as a part of his professional preparation for religious journalism. For nearly seven years at this writing, he has participated in a joyous venture of launching and nurturing a helpful journal of church recreation. Interestingly, there seems to be a particular quality of joy which he derives in making available to multiple thousands of well-and-strong people a vigorous program of recreation which, as a teen-ager, he missed. "Paralyzed, but productive" surely characterizes Larry Allison's life—so much so, in fact, that one is inclined to capitalize the whole word PRODUCTIVE in speaking of him.

Have you joined me in enjoying the drawings which have introduced various portions of this volume? Perhaps you would like to know *who* did them and *how* she did them.

She is *Nellie Faye Parker,* Georgia native, who suffered complete paralysis of arms and legs, including hand and feet, early in her life. Circumstances prevented her going to school, but her brothers and sisters shared with her their skills in reading and arithmetic. Within her handicapped body, however, there was the soul of an artist, and there was the latent skill to translate the inner motivation to drawing pad and canvas *with a brush held firmly between her teeth!*

Helpful friends and relatives in her home community gave encouragement and assistance, and a sojourn in the Georgia Rehabilitation Center in Warm Springs brought to her assistance additional instruction and inspiration. She has learned to do most creditable work in both oils and water-colors, and now she looks forward to a career in art. With genuine ability, high courage, and wonderful friends, Nellie Faye Parker is likely to paint her way to high success with that skilful brush between her teeth.

Incredible Triumph!

"Bachelor of Arts Degree, *Summa Cum Laude*," announced President Harold Tribble of Wake Forest College as *Martha Mason* was wheeled past by her devoted mother at spring degree-convocation on May 31, 1960. What was normal culmination of four years in college for the average collegian was a colossal triumph for this heroine of twelve years in an iron lung, now able to be out of the lung for only a few minutes with the aid of a portable lung worn unobserved beneath her bachelor's gown.

When polio "cast its vote" against Martha Mason in 1948, she was in the fifth grade of public school in North Carolina and already dreaming dreams of what she termed "years of gold" in college beyond her high school years. When news that Martha could live henceforth only if encased in an iron lung spread among friends and neighbors, there were, doubtless, some who felt that this lively, ambitious girl had received a knockout blow, and that the sadness of "it might have been" would be the atmosphere of the Mason home. If such were the thoughts of any of her townspeople, they sprang from an unawareness of the faith, courage, and ambition of this new iron lung resident!

For seven years of public school Martha was taught by unselfish teachers from the schools of her little Carolina community, aided by reading and conversations of admiring school friends. Her high courage and incredibly cheerful disposition made her home a bright spot for all of her school friends. Her capacity for scholarship, despite the great difficulties with which she had to cope, was never questioned by the admissions officials of the college to which she wished to go in her iron lung, because she graduated from high school with an all-time high average for that school of 98.6!

Physically infirm, but spiritually and psychologically strong, Martha did go to college! She and her parents occupied an apartment in the ground floor of a dormitory, and Martha "attended" classes, chapel, and church with the assistance of two-way communications. She recited as often as any other students, she took all the tests and examinations, she made all the book reports, and prepared all the term papers required in the classes in which she was registered. Neither asking nor accepting favors beyond the privilege of attending classes in her unique way, Martha Mason graduated from Gardner-Webb Junior College with a 96+ average for her two years. Thereafter any university in America would have felt honored to have her in its student body! Wake Forest College won the honor of her attendance.

"But, Martha, even if you do succeed in getting through college, don't submit yourself to the great possibility of deep disappointment by holding on to your long-time dream of becoming a journalist," a misguided would-be counselor might have volunteered. Sustained by her tremendous faith, emboldened by the supposedly impossible achievements of her college years, and inspired by the sure consciousness that some of the world's greatest writing has been done by people whose bodies were broken, blinded, and even crushed, Martha Mason did not turn in her dream.

By the time you read these lines, it is entirely possible that you will have read some article in a paper or magazine of national circulation with the glorious by-line, *Martha Mason!*

Company D: M.D.'S, Muscular Dystropsy, That Is!

Among the many different fraternities of the handicapped are some wonderful ones whom we may well call "Masters of Muscular Dystrophy." These delightful people, though permanently in the grip of an illness which causes a slow paralysis of muscles, have written a bright page in American life.

Though they are numerous in count and heroic in achievement, let us say hello to only two representatives of these valiant people.

Edward Canfield, of New York originally and later of Florida, was touched by muscular dystrophy at an early age. In the slow, but inexorable movement of the paralysis of muscles he became increasingly less agile in the use of arms and legs. For many years at this writing, he has been confined to bed, unable to walk or to sit up in a wheelchair, his legs now completely useless and his arms and hands partially impaired.

But, as so often happens when physical activity is impaired, the creative mind and courageous heart of Edward Canfield increased in vigor. While facing, on one hand, the knowledge that medical science has not yet found either prevention or cure for muscular dystrophy, he faced, on the other hand, the knowledge that many people with little or no physical strength have carved out careers of usefulness. Impelled by such conviction and courage, he has established a business of wide appeal in greeting cards and related items.

In one of his friendly mail outs, Edward Canfield said, "I do appreciate your friendly hand. I wish I could shake it and say thank you in person. . . ." In reading those words, the purchaser-reader had the stimulating feeling that he had reached across the miles for a handshake-in-spirit with a victorious man for whom even a physical handshake is next to impossible!

Whatever can a twelve-year-old girl accomplish if muscular dystrophy withdraws her from school with no more than the sixth grade completed? There would be no more classes with grand pals and wonderful teachers. There would be no more piano lessons as the quiet, but stilling touch of the illness crept onward. There would be no more sports activities or drama participation or camping with the Girl Scouts. Must one "throw in the sponge," cry with bitter disappointment, and simply "dry up" into uselessness? Though multiple hundreds in similar circumstances have voiced a vigorous no to that question, no one of that gallant group has replied in the negative with more success than has *Elsie Mangum Gunter* of Mississippi.[4]

Though permanently chair-bound from shortly after her twelfth birthday in years prior to the now-prevalent practice of making public school possible for people who do not walk or who walk with great difficulty, Elsie recognized that education is, in the final analysis, the continuing process of learning, and that nothing except lack of desire or determination could rob her of an excellent education. She began to read with wide scope of interest and with increasing sharpness of perception. She listened to excellent music on radio and records, often having in hand guidebooks to assist her in understanding more fully the message of the symphony or opera. She developed a more than ordinary talent for drawing soon after she became chair-bound, and years of subsequent study brought her to a point of professional skill as an artist.

Today she has as generous education in the liberal arts as most people achieve with master of arts degrees. Her knowledge of literature, drama, music, sociology, history, and psychology constantly amazes even the people who have been professionally trained in those fields. She is highly conversant with the great symphonies and with grand opera. Her greatest achievement, however, is in the field of art, in which she has found eminent success as a painter and as a teacher. Her imagination and creativity have inspired hundreds of students and other friends.

More recently, love and marriage have shed a bright and wonderful new light upon life—marriage to one with the soul of an artist and the skill of an engineer—and a whole new world of artistic insight has opened to her.

Joining Edward Canfield and Elsie Mangum Gunter in this company of "Masters of Muscular Dystrophy" are many others who, like these two, have faced the choice between roads—sorrowful, soul-withering self-pity and withering resignation to a life of inactivity, on the one hand: resilient, soul-stirring acceptance of the tremendous challenge to turn a handicap into victory, on the other hand—and who, like these two distinguished representatives of their fraternity, have chosen the highway of courage and victory. All hail to these M.D.V.'s, for they have routed the menace of muscular dystrophy with the "V" for victory spirit!

BATTALION TWO

Company A: The Blind Who See

"The truly blind people are not those whose eyes are darkened," remarked a shrewd observer, "but those whose souls are blind to what their eyes can see." In that fine sense, the heroes and heroines in this section of our parade are not blind at all; for, indeed, as we shall see, they have "seen" with minds alert and souls discerning to a degree which puts the eye-seeing ones of us to shame.

The victories of these valiant ones are particularly heroic ones, because they must adjust themselves to a world which talks almost incessantly about what it has seen; they must achieve education under handicaps which would defeat the less-than-brave; they must compete for success in their careers with competitors who see. Despite these mountains of difficulty, the ones who march before us now in this company of the parade have achieved education of quality, have succeeded admirably in school and career pursuits, and most of them have achieved great happiness in marriage.

Platoon 1: Born Sightless

The group passing immediately before us at this moment are people who were born with blindness or who lost sight in infancy. You would think, however, that they have seen all the colors of the spectrum, for they live such colorful lives. There is *Miss Margie Lou Presley*, for instance. She is totally blind in one eye, and she can see no more with the other eye than colors and dim outlines of objects. After graduation from the Texas School for the Blind, she took special training in medical terminology and case histories. Her mother read items in the field of medical materials to her, and she transcribed them into Braille for continuing study. Upon completion of her training, she obtained a position in a Dallas hospital's medical records department, and was soon transcribing between 9,000 and 12,000 words a day, listening to a dictaphone and using an electric typewriter. She lives alone in her Dallas apartment, plays piano and organ. It was no surprise to her friends when the Soroptimist Club of Dallas conferred upon her its 1962 Hurdle Award "in recognition of outstanding achievement through untiring courage and faith."

"YOUTH EXTENDS SIGHTLESS WORLD," announced a headline of an Associated Press article from Talladega, Alabama, in a recent year, and the article told of the stimulating exploit of *Larry Green*. Larry, at the time only eleven years of age, was the youngest blind applicant ever processed for the Federal Communications Commission license necessary for the "ham" operation of a shortwave radio. The article reported that Larry's call number, WN4IHI, was achieving a widening scope of contact with other operators and that in the first weeks of his operation of his 75-watt receiver-transmitter, he had reached 15 stations.

A helpful friend from the Talladega Radio Club, Otis Holmes, assisted Larry in his preparation for the writer's examination required for the license. This friend paid to Larry this splendid compliment: "I believe he picked up the code and other necessary radio knowledge faster than the average person who can see. . . . In tuning his transmission equipment, he goes by the sound of his receiver rather than by a meter. . . . Larry keeps a Braille log of his transmission, and crystals for his radio are marked in Braille."

The courageous determination of the "seeing blind" to participate in as many "sighted" activities as possible has been demonstrated by many of our sightless friends, of whom *Leah Russell* of Florida and *Fred Rader* of Kentucky are typical. During her high school days in Miami, Leah studied piccolo for three years, translating the music into Braille. At first, she was welcomed into the band of her high school only as a "sitting member." Her eagerness to join the marching band led her director to improvise a plan whereby bell players walked to her right and left, aiding her supersensitive hearing with whispered directions when right or left turns were in order. A compassionate, dedicated director plus

Leah's own patience and determination brought a challenging victory to a wonderful girl and a thrill to the thousands who saw her in marches during high school days. An Associated Press article reported her ambition for the future in these words: "Someday I will become a teacher and perhaps help other boys and girls to march in the dark."

Fred Rader did not believe that blindness necessarily excluded him from athletic events; therefore, he competed in discus, shot-put, and dashes during his high school years. His principal, Clark E. Chestnut, wrote these splendid words in a personal letter to me:

It was in the dashes that Fred showed the most courage, because of the fear of falling. He took his share of the falls, but always he came back for more.

He accomplished the discus and shot-put without too much trouble, but the dash was another story. We put Fred with a running mate who had a light rope about four or five feet long. Fred would hold the other end of the rope and would keep his direction by keeping the slack out of the rope. . . .

Fred also participated in speech events. He won a superior rating in discussion in the regional meet and got to the state contests. He received rating of "Good" in the state contests.

In the annual Kentucky High School Association Banquet in Louisville, Kentucky, in the spring of his senior year, Fred received the coveted "Game Guy Award," with the plaudits of the banqueteers and the multiple thousands who read of his courage in the newspapers.

Dr. Sam M. Lawton

In the company of the admirable ones who came into our world bereft of the gift of sight, there is no more heroic one than *Dr. Sam M. Lawton* of South Carolina. His academic degrees reveal accomplishments which would have been heroic for the sighted ones of us: bachelor of arts, graduate in theology, master of arts, and doctor of philosophy, the last-named degree being the highest academic degree conferred by American universities. All along the way of those arduous and accomplishing years, he did his outstanding work by listening intelligently in classes, by listening carefully as others read to him, and by a skilful use of his typewriter. Accepting no favors, he took all examinations and did all research papers on his typewriter.

Thanks to very wise parents, he came to believe that he could play games and accomplish achievements as well as his seeing friends, but that devising methods by which to accomplish these things was his responsibility. And, indeed, his brilliant record of achievements proves that he has translated that belief into victorious action. Here are some of his outstanding contributions: cofounder and first dean of instruction of North Greenville Junior College, college teacher and pastor in several college centers, contributor and strengthener to student religious movements sponsored by his denomination, travel and study abroad, wide popularity as lecturer in serious and humorous topics, founder of the South Carolina Aurora Club of the Blind (whose purpose is the spiritual and social growth of the blind), presidency of the National Church Conference of the Blind, and a coveted listing in *Who's Who of South Carolina.*

One of the most significant contributions which Dr. Lawton has made, if not the most significant, is his almost incredibly great usefulness for many years now as a University of South Carolina teacher in the off-campus centers of the university. He travels by bus, generally unaccompanied, to

five or more such centers each week; and in these wonderful
years has taught hundreds of students in Bible, psychology,
and other subjects, bringing to them a wealth of insights
beyond the textual information.

Added to the many citations which adorn his record is
the 1965 Piedmont Sertoma Club Award for "Service to
Mankind." The news accounts epitomized the feelings of
many thousands of Dr. Lawton's admirers:

His selection does honor to the award. . . . Dr. Lawton, blind since
birth, has distinguished himself as minister, educator, humanitarian.
He works constantly toward the improvement and inspiration of his
fellowman.

To know him and to be in his presence is to feel a warm glow about
humanity and its higher destiny.

No more appropriate honor to any more deserving person could have
been conceived.[5]

And do you know who that lovely woman is, standing in
the wings, smiling with joy, asking no credit for Dr. Lawton's accomplishments? She is his beloved wife, Alice, who
has been to him a masterful mosaic of love, devotion,
patience, courage, and helpfulness in a thousand ways.
Without her, Dr. Lawton's roster of achievements would be
shorter in length and less in luster!

Platoon 2: Blindness Called Later

A lively debate could be provoked, doubtless, concerning
the comparative disadvantage of blindness from birth and
blindness after years of sight. But, regardless of the out-
come of such debates, there are those upon whom blindness
called after years of normal sight who have shown high

courage in readjustment. One such hero is *Jimmy Martindale*, concerning whom a news writer in his city did an article with the title "*A STUDY IN COURAGE. . . . Jimmy Martindale: The Lad Who Refused to Quit When Fate Dealt Him Tragedy.*"[6]

Jimmy and a Boy Scout pal were preparing for an outing; and, as is customary with early teen-age boys, their preparations had various interruptions for examinations of "how things work." In one such examination of a shotgun, there was a miscue, and the ensuing blast ripped off one of Jimmy's fingers and sent him into the world of blindness, though not into a world of despair. Local clubs, individuals, and a host of personal friends came to his side in a heartwarming display of feeling and responsibility for helping a youth to overcome his handicap. A seeing-eye dog, completion of education through undergraduate and graduate degrees, and inevitable success in his chosen vocation are some of the proofs that a seeing individual can make a magnificent adjustment to the new world of darkness.

Marcia Setzer of Missouri was already busily and happily engaged in a teaching career when she learned from doctors that her diabetic condition had developed complications which would lead to eventual blindness. Instead of succumbing to self-pity, fear, or hysteria, she faced the future with the confident conviction that she could and would adjust to blindness *without giving up teaching as a career*.

She took additional courses in a local university and spent four months in a rehabilitation center. She learned to travel with confidence through the use of the white cane, to look after all the personal needs of an independent existence, to use Braille effectively in study and typewriting, to use a tape recorder for assignments, and to do a multitude of little things essential to daily living. Upon her completion of these preparations, she obtained a position as teacher of French and Spanish in an excellent high school in her state. For Marcia Setzer, blindness became simply *an unexpected mountain* in the pathway of her life and career; but, instead of turning back to look for another or easier way, she acted in the highest tradition of the courageous mountain-climber, and, indeed, she has "climbed every mountain."

The doctors had told *Dale Kirkland,* a rural mail carrier and a man of splendid education and refinement, that he would lose his eyesight, and that the loss would probably be a sudden occurrence. With a head full of preparation and a heart full of faith, he continued his rural mail route with happiness and high humor.

As he traveled his route one day, the blindness came with the suddenness about which he had been told. He knew the road so well, that he simply drove his car to the roadside and waited. A passing friend paused to enquire of his trouble, and Mr. Kirkland replied in resilient spirit, "My lights have just gone out."

The descent of total blindness did not find Dale Kirkland unprepared. Upon his arrival home that afternoon, he went into his room and, kneeling to pray, he asked God to help him to surmount his handicap—not just for himself, but for a sister in college to whom he was greatly devoted.

As have so many courageous ones whose pattern of life has changed with dramatic suddenness, Dale Kirkland asked no more than an opportunity to make his way in some new activity. From his own wide readings and magazine contacts, it was easy for him to warm up to magazine salesmanship.

Despite his suitability to his new work and his enthusiasm for it, the going was rough for him so often in those early months and years. On one of those early days his sales netted one dollar! With determination, resourcefulness, and never-absent good humor he stayed with his job. In a recent year his sales were phenomenal, and he has become one of America's most successful men in that field.

Though his eyes do not see, his bright mind is so alert and perceptive that even his fingers seem to have eyes. For instance, he makes very beautiful precision clocks which rival the work of the excellent clock and cabinet makers of Switzerland and Germany. His Arkansas home is worth a trip of considerable length to see: it combines the colonial with the modern into a marvelous picturesqueness, and visitors there are agreed that the atmosphere of the Kirkland home gives one a sense of culture, beauty, hospitality, and a stimulating impression of courageous, victorious Christian living.

The light of the candle of courage in the heart of Dale Kirkland was caught by the life of the sister, for whose college education he was so concerned. After graduation from two great universities, travel in Europe, and twenty years of college teaching she became totally blind. She and her mother, whose one hundredth birthday was celebrated in 1961, shared the spacious and beautiful Kirkland home. Miss Kirkland's life continues to be one of tremendous usefulness in church and community; for she, too, has had the courage to accept a changed role and vocation with the resourcefulness of a mind filled with preparation and a heart illumined by faith and intelligent surrender.

There are none so blind as those who, though they have eyes, do not see; there are none so seeing as those who, though they be physically blind, can see with eyes of a faith-filled heart and a courage-filled life!

Platoon 3: These Knew No Limits

Although *courage* is the hallmark of the entire company of those who make up this section of our parade of valiant ones who wouldn't quit, some of this group have proved that the impossible is possible if courage is deep enough, dedication is high enough, and patience is long enough. Notice *Miss Tommie Goins,* for instance. See the companion walking with her, working her fingers rapidly in Tommie's hand? The explanation is simply this: Tommie is both blind and deaf, and the companion is "talking" into her hand with touch interpretations of what is going on. Notice the rich variety of expressions on Tommie's face? She understands quickly and fully what her interpreter is "saying," and she is actually talking back to her interpreter with vocal expressions!

Although Tommie Goins' versatility gives to her a personality so distinctive that she can hardly be compared, her dual handicap reminds one immediately of Helen Keller. The "Anne Sullivans" of Tommie's life to date have been a beloved grandmother, a discerning rehabilitation counselor, and several helpful college mates.

Thanks to wonderful home training, happy acceptance in the community in which she grew up, superlatively fine help from the School for the Blind in her home state of Mississippi, and the mature continuing counsel of her adult counselor, she had no fears in applying for acceptance in college. Intense examinations of every relevant type in Syracuse University resulted in her being awarded one of the coveted Helen Keller scholarships—the first student in the South and only the fifth in the nation ever to receive that scholarship award.

Blue Mountain College, near her home city, was her

choice of college, and she was accepted there. With the aid of a full-time companion to interpret, and with the joyous warmth of affection and admiration which the students of the college gave to her, she achieved an outstanding record in her college years. On May 29, 1966, she received the bachelor of arts degree with a very high quality point average and with the thunderous applause of a large and admiring audience. In receiving her degree, she became the first deaf-blind student in the South ever to complete a full four-year college course.

Because she talks audibly with amazing clarity and beautiful enunciation, with the interpreter's hand impressions conveying the "other half" of any conversation, she can carry on an animated conversation; and, on the day of her graduation from college, she told all enquirers of her happiness in being accepted for graduate study in English and of her aspiration to become a teacher. Those who know Tommie Goins entertain no doubt that she will prove conclusively that whatever is said to be impossible for her will become only another challenge accepted and conquered!

Jane and *Avery Dotson,* husband and wife and both blind, have given living proof that the highest level of scholarship, the happiest adjustment in marriage, and the finest of creative contribution to life can be made by sightless people. Sweethearts since being fellow students in the Kentucky School for the Blind, Jane and Avery married after graduation. With her expert typing ability, she became the breadwinner while Avery completed his university degree. With his degree completed and a position obtained in occupational therapy in a Veteran's Administration Hospital, Avery became the breadwinner while Jane proceeded to Cincinnati University. Not only did she take her degree with honors, but, also, was initiated into Phi Beta Kappa, America's top-level scholarship group.

A reporter spoke glowingly of the Dotsons as Jane's graduation approached.[7] Among other stimulating insights to the Dotsons' life and philosophy shared by the reporter were these delightful items:

> "We have a motto," said Jane. "It is up to us, as blind who are in the minority, to adjust to the sighted world who are in the majority." One of her goals is to see blind children integrated into sighted classes at start of school.

> "The Dotsons keep lights on in the house all evening," Jane said. "We don't want to be the only dark house on the street." And she said they often eat dinner by candlelight, adding "We love atmosphere. We can sense it."

Reporting that the leisure-time activities of the Dotsons includes television, and asking the reason, the reporter received this delightful reply: "The majority of our friends are sighted. We wouldn't want to blind TV for them."

And, so, this gallant company of "The Blind Who See" passes our reviewing stand, leaving us with a commixture of sentiments, one of which is this: *we who are sighted may well be more handicapped than they; for, indeed, so many of us who LOOK, seem not to SEE!*

BATTALION THREE

Company A: Bed-bound, but Boundless.

Wouldn't it be interesting, if not amazing, to hear individuals handicapped in different ways in a discussion of the advantages of their particular handicaps over the handicaps borne by other people? And the wonderful down-but-not-out constituents of this volume would be discussing *advantages,* not *disadvantages!* If such a discussion were to occur, we can be sure that those confined permanently to their beds would be among the most eloquent in presenting their claims to advantage; for, wonderful to say, so many of them have turned their bed-bound status into a boundless source of inspiration and strength to the well-and-strong— some of whom came to comfort the bed-bound, but who went away comforted.

I have stood and sat at the bedsides of some of this company and can attest that, though their bodies were bound to beds, their hearts and influence knew no boundaries. I recall a radiant woman who performed a vital telephone ministry from her bed each day: she called many people in behalf of her church, and she performed a personal ministry of courage and consolation in telephone conversations with people in her area who faced difficulties. I remember, too, the heroic woman who was touched by blindness and paralysis after busy and fruitful years of normal living, but who dedicated her abed-years to a ministry of prayer in behalf of the growing number of people who sought her prayer help. I remember two men in the same city, one bed-bound for many years by a slow-moving and incurable malady, and the other bed-bound by a malignancy which nibbled at his body until that body had become a virtual "stump" of body. From the bedsides of both men, however, there flowed a constant stream of optimism, humor, high courage, and victory. People in their city who were well and strong were reluctant to complain of difficulty when the thought of these bed-bound, but boundless men came to their hearts.

For seven years *Bill Cain* of Houston, Texas, was confined to his bed, that is, except for times in which he continued his battle against polio and complications in an iron lung.

To this lad's bedroom there came a constant stream of visitors. They came to solace and to cheer, but more likely they left having received far more than they brought. For this bedroom was not a place of sorrow or of frustration or of defeat. Here was zest for life, gaiety, the aura of high courage. The uninitiated visitor might come with softened step. . . . He would leave with bold step and uplifted heart, for he had been in the presence of the conquest of the spirit.

The visitors who came were children of the neighborhood, lovely ladies of Hollywood, stars of stage and screen, movie cowboys, wrestlers and pugilists, newspapermen, musicians, doctors—and preachers.[8]

Among the preachers who came was a distinguished seminary president. Bill had heard through his church of the seminary's desire to build a chapel on campus. Although the seminary president had called upon Bill merely to have touch with this gallant spirit, he was overwhelmed when Bill surprised him with the insistence that the president accept $35.00 which he had saved from his weekly allowance. This twentieth-century version of the famous New Testament "widow's mite" touched the president's heart to tears, and the news of it touched the hearts of alumni of Southern Baptist Seminary in Louisville, Kentucky. In the now-completed chapel, there is a BILL CAIN ROOM, the office of the dean of students; and from this vital office of counsel, guidance, and strength there continues to flow the same spirit of victory which flowed in a constant stream from Bill's bedside in Houston some years ago. Bill Cain's bed in Houston is vacant now, because the experience which men call death conveyed him to a land and life without limitations; yet, his influence continues to move among people around the world through the lives of seminary students who have found strength and challenge in the seminary room named in his honor.

Bill Cain's triumphant life brings to mind a wonderful *Virginia lad* who was totally paralyzed, but from whose bright mind so many clever gadgets for improving the handling of his inert body arose, that visitors were intrigued and delighted in visits to his bedroom and went away challenged to find creative solutions to their problems. . . . And a lovely *Alabama woman*, living adjacent to a college campus, who gave counsel, courage, and inspiration to several generations of collegians—all from her bed, upon which her crippled and withered body lay inert.

A Stimulating Story

Some years ago, *Guideposts* shared the stimulating story of *Gerber D. Schafer*, a disabled veteran of World War I, who had spent 24 years "flat on his back, unable to move a muscle below his chin," and who had spent 15 years at that time in a Pennsylvania hospital. Overcoming the shock of total infirmity, responding to the generous interest of throngs of people who wrote to him, and discovering that he could raise money over telephone and through news articles to help other people with handicaps, he had become a veritable "Good Samaritan" to many shut-ins and others who needed help of varying kinds.

Nurses put the telephone receiver to his ear and dialed calls for him; volunteer secretaries rejoiced to work for him; people of all walks felt honored to cooperate with his projects; a steady throng of people came and went. Every time he was able to arrange for the help which someone needed, according to *Guideposts'* article, he closed his eyes for a moment and said, "Dear God, thank you for giving me this chance to help another shut-in."[9]

Determination, courage, unselfishness, and complete devotion of a wonderful wife explain the phenomenal achievement of the late *Clarence E. Power* of Marietta, Georgia. When the doctors found that he had the same physical ailment which removed the great Lou Gehrig of baseball fame, they indicated to him that he would never sit up again and, perhaps, would have less than a month of life, he declined to "throw in the sponge." Instead, he prayed fervently for strength and courage to survive, hoping thereby to bring strength and cheer to shut-ins far and near. For over a quarter of a century he did survive, and he did bring strength and cheer to multiple thousands of shut-ins throughout America.

Earning a part of his livelihood through a brisk sale of greeting cards, magazine subscriptions, and renewals, Clarence "Billy" Power became nationally known through his vast correspondence with other shut-ins. To them he sent words of cheer, poems, and other quotations which relighted burned-out candles of hope in many hearts. A host of newspaper columnists, radio personalities, and ministers assisted in his favorite project—to establish the first Sunday in June as International Shut-ins Day, on which day people were urged to visit shut-ins in their communities. So widely did his triumphant philosophy spread, that he became known throughout the nation as "The Sunshine Man"; to him the mighty and the great paid tribute, while he gave thanks to God and to his wonderful wife for their assistance in his effort to turn his bed-bound status into victory and blessing for himself and others. Although he has gone, the lengthened shadow of his useful life lives on in the lives of other people who are sharing sunshine from their invalid couches and in the international observance of "Shut-In Sunday" every June.

Under the title of "The Most Unforgettable Character I've Met," *Reader's Digest* carried a well-written article by Anne Morrow Lindbergh concerning *Edward Sheldon*. Mr. Sheldon had been an eminently successful playwright, but had been bed-bound for twenty years with paralysis and blindness. After describing his meteoric rise to great fame in the theatrical world while still in his late twenties, Mrs. Lindbergh described his physical plight in these graphic words:

He was first lamed, then crippled and confined to a wheelchair, and finally frozen in rigidity, imprisoned in bed for life. As if this were not more than one human frame could bear, in his late 30's he became blind as well.[10]

As his life drew near its earthly conclusion, even his voice threatened to cease functioning; but, filled with resourcefulness, Edward Sheldon planned to learn the Morse code and to communicate with friends through telegraphic signals. This last resource he did not have to use: for, as death called for him, he was still able to communicate in spoken word, though in somewhat breathless manner.

Just as joyously and creatively as he had gone out to meet life and the world, both life and the world came to him when he was bed-bound. He seemed to forget himself completely and to lose himself so thoroughly in the lives of whatever individuals were in his room, that those individuals felt that they were the most important people in the world to Edward Sheldon. In hours of counsel with other playwrights and people of all levels of vocation and materials he gave himself so totally that all who visited him went out of his room with a mystical feeling of complete well-being. Mrs. Lindbergh sensed that many who visited Edward Sheldon could say: "He understood me; nobody understood me so well."

Through telegrams, letters, and messages through individuals, he followed out into the world those who had spent some time with him in his invalid quarters, surprising them with the effectiveness and unselfishness of his memory, amazing them that he spoke of spring and autumn and life and color as if his blinded eyes could see. Mrs. Lindbergh concluded her stirring article with this discerning summary:

Have I come back then to the oversimplified conclusion that Edward Sheldon was a saint? . . . If the word *saint* be taken as a symbol for an ordinary man who had overcome superhuman difficulties in his own life; who, after overcoming them still had ardor enough left to give to those he came in contact with; whose vision was so sharpened by suffering and illuminated by love that he saw everyone as they were meant to be; and, finally, a man who lived a large proportion of his life in a world of eternal values, free of the pressures of time and fear, greed and passion—yes, then it might be said that Edward Sheldon filled the symbol of sainthood.

To borrow the title of a popular semireligious number of our day, "When the Saints Go Marching In," there will be many of those saints who achieved a sainthood similar to that conferred upon Mr. Sheldon by Mrs. Lindbergh in the way in which Mr. Sheldon achieved it—by a creative acceptance of a bed-bound existence, by a losing of themselves in the lives of others, and by a finding of both joy and usefulness which their days of physical health had not brought to them. Indeed, these wonderful ones are and have been *bedbound, but boundless!*

Company B: The Queen's Court

In deference to our American addiction to choosing a queen for every event, your author has presumed to choose a queen for these three inspiring battalions of our parade of the down-but-not-out heroes and heroines. In the conviction that a queen should embody the best ideals of the groups which she represents, that she should possess the grace and charm traditionally associated with the queenship, and that she should have the capacity for evoking deep devotion and high inspiration, I present *Ruth Landes Pitts*, native Texan, but with the whole wide world in her joyous heart.

No prettier bride than Ruth Landes ever walked down a church aisle. On that September night in 1961, a thousand hearts of admiring friends were loving her, admiring her, and wishing for her even greater happiness than the superlatively happy years which had preceded this significant evening. As Ruth's father, the distinguished pastor of the church in which she was being married, waited to perform the ceremony, and as her devoted mother looked through a heart large with love and through understandable tears of nostalgia and joy in the daughter's marriage to a magnificent young man, the vast congregation felt a sense of tremendous drama.

You see, Ruth would have been called by the casual observer a "handicapped person"; but if weights had ever become wings, they had surely done so in this glorious young woman's life. She was born in 1939 physically afflicted in both hands and in both feet. The unthinking or unimaginative might have sighed with the sad prediction, "Poor child, she will never be able to do much with her hands or feet!" It is to be hoped that any such prophets have kept up with Ruth Landes in these succeeding years.

Thanks to the wisdom of parents and the response of a very bright mind, Ruth never regarded her limitations as a handicap; rather, she thought of them as a stimulating challenge to overcome. That she has achieved an unending succession of brilliant victories is eloquently proved by the records. Though, perhaps, very few people with her severe handicaps would have dared to study piano, studying piano was one of the several challenges which Ruth accepted. Co-operating wonderfully with a discerning piano teacher, Ruth became a brilliant pianist. With good basic ability in voice she achieved unusually high honors in both high school and college in choral groups; and, never succumbing to the lure of the easier way, she took her college degree in music education.

Along the way of high school and college years Ruth achieved a roster of honors in student activity that dazzle both the eye and imagination. The average "Who's Who" publication could allow space for hardly half of the scintillating honors which came to this radiant, victorious girl.

Though there are times in which handicapped people have been content to rest upon some achievements with the feeling, "I've shown myself and others that I *can* do things," Ruth Landes proved that her high school and college achievements were not mere "window dressings" for a desire to prove that she could achieve. Graduating from college in three years *cum laude,* she received a three-year fellowship from the National Defense Education Act. In less than a year she received a master's degree as one of three students in a graduating class of 600 acclaimed as "demonstrating those characteristics of heart and mind and conduct which evince a spirit of love to others."

At this writing, Ruth is approaching her doctorate, teaching with happiness and success in a college in the university center, and having the greatest joy of all in the presence of a precious little son in her home. When, as anticipated, she receives the doctorate in the course of 1967, she is sure to be acclaimed again as the fulfilment of the educators' dreams for the perfect student. The superb young man whom Ruth married that September night in 1961 was a graduate student in the same university center. He, too, is approaching his doctorate and will teach in a distinguished university in the Southeast.

So great has been Ruth's victory over handicaps that the concourse of her friends pay her the rarest of all compliments to the handicapped: "We never think of Ruth as handicapped; in fact, we would be happily willing to have her handicaps if we could have, too, her magnificent spirit of joyous victory!"

NOTES

1. Quoted by staff writer Dolores Lescure in *Richmond News-Leader* as part of a series of articles on personalities of the Richmond, Virginia, school system.

2. Personal communication from Wade Bryant, distinguished minister.

3. Dolores Lescure, *op. cit.*

4. She did the design from which the front jacket was taken.

5. *Spartanburg Herald*, May 15, 1965.

6. Robert Palmer, *Texarkana Gazette*, March 26, 1960.

7. Libby Lackman in *The Cincinnati Enquirer*, June 17, 1960.

8. Editor Coleman Craig in *The Baptist Review*, November-December, 1959.

9. *Guideposts*, January, 1947, pp. 1ff.

10. *Reader's Digest*, January, 1947, p. 1 ff.

Masters of Mosaic:

3 JOB'S CHILDREN

"We are handicapped on all sides, but we are never frustrated," [1] would be a superlatively appropriate inscription for the shields of a battalion of victorious people into whose lives many difficulties have come. Their hardships multiplied, their disappointments were many, their sorrows were compounded; yet, they never permitted even this multiplication of difficulties to handicap their spirit of victory.

These remarkable people remind us of Job and his experiences. In rapid succession, three messengers came rushing to Job to tell him of tragedies which had come to his material possessions; and, while the third messenger was relating his message of loss, the fourth messenger arrived to tell Job of the death of his children in a windstorm. Even so, this good, great man worshipped God and did not accuse God foolishly. In addition to these heartbreaking losses, Job lost his health and became a mass of boils. Resisting even the loss of faith on the part of his wife and the limited thinking of his "comforters," Job stood steadfastly on his faith in God.

It is my hope that readers with less to handicap them than these presented here have had, may read their stories with embarrassment at any lack of courage, and may be challenged to look again at their own handicaps. It is my hope, too, that readers with as many difficulties as these will read of their victories with joy and with resolution to make of their own mountains of difficulty a pathway of victory.

First, meet a wonderful man who was chosen "Handicapped Man of the Year" in his state recently. Because of handicaps which might have defeated a man of lesser courage, he has had three careers, going from one to another as doors closed. In his teens and early twenties he was a professional boxer. Rheumatoid arthritis struck his strength, and he was obliged to relinquish a career in which he had experienced joy and success. But he was not "counted out."

After a time of recuperation, he became a boxing coach. Transmitting his know-how, spirit of enthusiasm, and high courage to the teams he coached in the state university of his state, he produced some of the nation's top boxing teams. At the peak of this career, he was brought down again by disease and was confined to his bed for six years. But the referees didn't count him out on this second round: they knew his courage!

During his long confinement, he studied and took training to become an accountant; and, for seventeen years prior to his receiving the top handicap award in his state, he had worked as a valuable and successful employee in an important government finance division. And, though it is to be hoped by all who know him and by those of us who read his story that no other handicap will knock at his door, it is easy to predict that he would conquer that unwanted caller too!

A Lady of the Deep South

Now, meet this completely lovely and gracious woman of the deep South; and, after admiring the almost unparalleled radiance of her face, sparkle of her eyes, and zest of her spirit, sit down with me to greater admiration and thrill in hearing her story. Although she has said to me, "Oh, I haven't done anything special," I feel that she is one of the most magnificent of "Job's children."

Every mother can enter into the high and holy expectations which this splendid woman experienced at the approach of the birth of the first child of her marriage. The glad day came, but the little boy received a birth injury which made impossible his walking, talking, or taking care of himself in any way. Some mothers who read these lines will know, too, of the depth of sorrow in this young mother's heart in realizing that this would be her only hope of a child of her own.

It is probable that some would-be helpers suggested that the child be sent to an institution in which he could be attended and supervised hour by hour; but, if such counsel came, it was smiled away by the loving dedication of this quiet little woman who resolved to keep this wee morsel of wounded humanity close to her heart and arms. And so she has kept him—for forty-seven years at the time of this writing. For thirty-two of those years, the lad had numerous convulsions daily—from twenty-five to thirty on some days. When the convulsions subsided, it was found that his heart was in dangerous condition. This valiant woman's faith has never wavered; the smile has never left her face; a song of praise to God for the opportunity of life and service has been on her lips perpetually.

You are thinking, perhaps, "That's enough to break anybody's health and heart." But that is not all! Nineteen years after the little son's birth, this woman of valor faced another grave crisis: her husband suffered a stroke which left him unable to speak or walk. On wings of song and love, she read the eyes of this man she loved so much, interpreted and met his needs, and kept the fragrance of happiness all around him for more than twelve years . . . until his death.

When I visited this heroine of the crucible one day, her aged, bedridden, deaf mother was recuperating from a broken hip and was the latest recipient of her daughter's devotion and love. The daughter *wanted so much* to minister to her mother's needs, and to bring as much happiness as possible in the sunset hours of her life. This chapter of love and devotion to her bedridden mother continued for seven years, but nothing of complaint was heard from the daughter's lips; there was only gratitude that she had the privilege of making these years comfortable ones for a beloved mother!

If all of those things had happened to you, would you have felt that the church would just have to get along without you, that you could not possibly find time or energy to perform tasks there, and that everybody ought to understand that you could not be a serving member? This valorous woman's pastor has written to say that she is superintendent of a department in Sunday School, that the department meets the highest standards of accreditation, and that its functioning is a joy to behold.

Perhaps you feel as I do at this juncture: you feel the impulse to pause to thank God for a person like that, and to ask God to touch your life with a full measure of her courage, patience, unselfishness, and love . . . and her complete faith in the adequacy of God's power. She said smilingly to your author as he bade her good-bye, following a luncheon period, and as he complimented her upon the triumph of her life, "I don't really deserve any credit; I just claimed the promises of God's Word, and I have found them to be completely adequate."

This wonderful "Daughter of Job" brings to mind an expression of faith voiced by the English poet, Wordsworth, in his well remembered composition, "The Excursion":

> One adequate support
> For the calamities of mortal life
> Exists—one only: an assured belief
> That the procession of our fate, howe'er
> Sad or disturbed, is ordered by a Being
> Of infinite benevolence and power;
> Whose everlasting purpose embraces
> All accidents, converting them to good.

But this inspiring woman said it ever so much more simply in quoting, *"I can do all things through Christ which strengtheneth me"* (Phil. 4:13).

Next in the inspiring group of "Job's Children," those to whom much of sorrow and loss has come, is a striking man of age seventy-three, who, in a recent year, was named by the President's Committee on Employment of the Handicapped as "Handicapped American of the year." In an accident in his early years, he lost a large part of his right arm. Then, there came to him the loss of his voice from cancer of the vocal cords. Also, there came the loss of sight in one eye.

Following each of these potential tragedies, this heroic

man assessed his losses and his assets, and started all over again. After the loss of a part of his right arm, he returned to school to learn vocational skill to replace the work which he had done as an electrician prior to the loss of his arm. He began to achieve success in both salesmanship and part-time professional singing, but both of these activities had to be relinquished when cancer robbed him of his voice.

Not dissuaded or despairing from even these multiplying handicaps, increased still farther by the loss of sight in one eye, he studied arduously the technique of "esophageal speech" until he had mastered it. At the time of his receiving the national award, he had already taught more than 100 persons to speak, despite the loss of their vocal cords. He has come to be an authority in this significant field and is in great demand by Veterans Administration, general rehabilitation groups, and medical schools.

This wonderfully inspired fellow citizen of ours has proved as eloquently as anyone of my knowledge that there is victory for every handicap, regardless of the number which may come to any one individual—including, in this remarkable man's instance, the misclassified handicap of advancing age!

Inspiring Young Man

Now, let's meet an inspiring young man whose neither-down-nor-out spirit has thrilled many people. This young man's series of Job-like experiences began when he was two years of age. Bone cancer touched his limbs, and 135 operations ensued. When he was twenty-three, polio paid its call with these permanent reminders of its visit: both legs, his left arm, left side of his neck, and entire left side paralyzed. With radiance, courage, and determination he has lived

through these years of successive blows with a Job-like faith
which has not wavered.

This cavalcade of heroes and heroines of multiple difficulties and sorrows could go on and on with abiding inspiration
to those of us who have wrestled with even lesser handicaps,
but we could conclude it with no more magnificent illustration of this heroic group than that of the life of Mrs. Iona
Henry McLaughlin, whose story is told in the book, *Triumph
over Tragedy*.[2] A reading of this book is recommended to
those who feel that they have received too much of sorrow
and suffering.

Mr. and Mrs. Henry had suffered the anxiety of parents
who wait through days and nights of the serious illness of a
beloved child, and found themselves exhausted from physical weariness and grief when the lovely daughter died.
They decided to take some time off to visit Mr. Henry's
minister father in the West. After lodging overnight in an
Illinois motel, they breakfasted and resumed their journey.
They did not hear the approaching train; in the ensuing
crash Mr. Henry and the son lost their lives instantly. Mrs.
Henry, injured apparently beyond recovery, was admitted
to a nearby hospital, whose admittance sheet indicated her
blood pressure to be zero over zero.

Her heart was broken from the loss of husband, son, and
daughter. Her body was broken so badly that its recovery—
if ever it should occur—would take months and years. She
came to eventual consciousness. Then she had to fight tragic
battles with pain, the wish to die, fear, loneliness, and
months of wondering "Why did this happen, and why and
for what should I want to live?"

The saga of her return to the desire to live, her readjustment to life without those who meant most to her, her

resumption of higher education, and her eventual triumphant living on a college campus should prove to any whose lives have been broken to pieces, that a new life, though different, can be built from the pieces of the broken life.

Mosaics to Masterpieces

Near to Lake Wales, Florida, there is a tourist attraction called *The Great Masterpiece*. It is made up of 300,000 pieces of broken tile, put together to reproduce Da Vinci's immortal *Last Supper*.

At the outset of World War II this masterpiece, which was then in Germany, was dismantled and hidden underground to protect it from the ravages of war. It survived those tragic years; and, upon the conclusion of the war, it was brought to America—first to the Midwest, then to the West, and finally to Florida. There it has found a permanent home. As I have viewed this masterpiece on several occasions, my heart has received this message:

Though your *life* be broken into pieces, it, too, can be put back together by the hand of a master artist, so that the reassembly of the broken pieces may be even more inspiring to your world than the arrangement you had preferred. . . . But you will be wise to let that Master of the art of life and living do the putting of the pieces together; for only he has the wisdom, patience, power, and love to turn your broken life into a masterpiece of mosaic!

NOTES

1. 2 Corinthians 4:8, from *The New Testament in Modern English,* c J. B. Phillips, 1958. Used with permission of The Macmillan Company.

2. Iona Henry McLaughlin (with Frank Mead), *Triumph over Tragedy* (Nashville, Tenn.: Parthenon Press.) Mrs. Henry is now Dr. Iona Henry McLaughlin of Washington, D. C.

Demons and Angels:

4 DEMONS NO DOUBT!

In any moment of crisis or vicissitude, there are likely to be two tugs at the individual: an upward tug and a downward tug . . . the challenge to rise above self to a victory which satisfies and inspires, or the temptation to give way to selfishness and resentment into an attitude which condemns and destroys. It is not surprising, therefore, that the heroes of this book faced those two tugs. In referring to some factors which they had to fight, several of them spoke of "the demon of self-pity" and "the demon of fear." Also, they referred to the people and factors which helped them to victory as "angels of mercy." Hence, the title of this division arose, and the purpose of this section of our book is to examine the factors which hindered and those which helped our valiant ones to become neither down nor out. First, let's look through their heroic eyes at some of the "demons" which they confronted and conquered in their sagas of victory.

1. *Fear.*—One after another of our heroes of victory over handicaps indicated that their first, if not greatest victory after the coming of handicaps was the victory over fear. Many of them found the basis for their victory in the rich promises of God's Word and in the faith-filled appropriation of those promises through fervent prayer.

After maintaining a breathless vigil outside the quarters in which his younger daughter fought through her first night with bulbar polio, a devoted father epitomized his own fears and the later-confided fears of his daughter in these words:

I knew then, more than ever before, that polio was not so much a disease of pain as it was of fear, a silent, secret, impending fear. There is some terrible dread of the body's destruction, a destruction of some vital part of the self, and it is a sensation not easily conveyed to one not experiencing it.[1]

The brave daughter who fought the demon of fear through the first night gave her own wonderful testimony later: "I conquered polio that first night. . . . After that, it never again held so great a fear for me." [2]

An author who has entered often and deeply into the lives of suffering and handicapped people summarized the demon-potential of fear in these striking lines: "Fear, above all else, is the greatest destroyer. No disease can destroy as rapidly nor as completely as fear." [3]

One of our heroines, one who had virtually a "Job's portion" of difficulties, gave her testimony to the demonic power of fear in these words:

Fear is a sneak, an artist at the sneak attack. It hovers under cover of pain; it strikes in the dark, in low moments when you are least ready to meet it. And you fight it alone, inside. There are no drugs to conquer fear. Like pain, fear is inevitable. It comes to all of us, in one form or another. Whoever you are, wherever you are, some day you will have to meet it and beat it, unless you want it to beat you.

It can be beaten, if you are smart enough to accept the help of certain allies. Mature people who face their problems can whip fear if they want to.[4]

2. *Self-pity.*—No other tug to defeat in the face of a handicap has been more frequently or more thoroughly "demonized" than the demon of self-pity! Many of our handicapped victors have indicated that healing of heart or body simply did not begin until self-pity had been recognized and routed, and that they were often shocked to face up to the fact that what they had thought to be a rather noble "martyr" attitude was really self-pity.

One husband-wife team, facing the shocking discovery that their firstborn child was Mongoloid, went through an initial period of recrimination, doubts concerning God, and just plain heartsickness. Upon recognizing that they were really indulging in self-pity and not in pity for the handicapped child, their whole attitude changed, and the whole picture changed. Writing to a widely-read columnist, this husband-wife team said:

Our darling daughter is now 11 years old. She is the happiest, most affectionate, the sweetest child of all. We would not trade her for three normal children. She has taught us unselfishness and devotion. This little girl brought us a very special message. We would not have missed it for the world.[5]

From his many rich years of dealing with people whose lives have been hurt, Dr. Ted Adams pinpoints the real danger of self-pity in these piercing words: "Nothing is more dangerous to one's character and more intolerable for neighbors, friends, and loved ones than self-pity. Self-pity has no justification." [6]

Many of our victorious handicapped ones have found challenge, guidance, and strength from the example of Christ, who never felt sorry for himself, regardless of difficulties— even the cross. Speaking of Christ's victory over self-pity, one writer gave these words, which have aided many handicapped ones in their victories over self-pity: "Why, his first victory on the cross, the very beginning of his final victory— and ours, too—over all kinds of circumstances, was a victory over 'hurt feelings' and 'feeling sorry for himself!' " [7]

Speaking of the personality-wide damage which self-pity can do, the same author painted this graphic picture: "Hurt feelings blind you to reality. Why, when your feelings are hurt, they are like burns on the soul, liable to such deadly infections as *feeling sorry for yourself, resentment, anger, blame, suspicion, and fear*—infectious poisons which twist and destroy personality." [8]

3. *Selfishness.*—Some of the triumphant handicapped ones pointed out the probability that self-pity, not faced and conquered, would lead inevitably to a permanent state of attitude which only the word *selfishness* could convey accurately: the feeling that everybody round about should adjust to the whims of the handicapped one, that "since this has happened to me, it is your responsibility to help make up for my misfortune with special favors and attention." These conquering handicapped ones came to realize that the emotional and psychological suffering of people around them—particularly those nearest and dearest to them—was as great as that of the individuals to whom misfortune had come, that the close family and friends were "going out of their way and going the second and third miles" constantly,

and that the handicapped ones owed to these devoted associates an unselfishness of spirit which could make the load for all much lighter.

4. *Resentment.*—Resentment toward God because of a mistaken concept of God's dealings with his children, resentment toward individuals who may have figured in the coming of the handicap or hurt, resentment toward the people who try to help or heal, or just a general resentment toward everybody and everything have been emotions with which handicapped people have had to struggle; and, according to their testimonies, some of their richest victories have come in this struggle.

Several—and, perhaps, many others—found their way to victory through the example and teachings of Christ, who, despite the greatest hurt ever accorded an individual, did not permit resentment to take lodgment in his heart. These and others found help, too, in the splendid writings of good counselors. One such book which gave the way to victory over resentment to many was author Van Keuren's book, mentioned earlier. Two excellent passages of wide help are these concerning Christ on the cross:

Suppose he had let thoughts of blame, resentment, and even revenge fill his mind. Suppose he had indulged in feeling sorry for himself. Don't you see, he would then have made not only his body but his soul vulnerable to them? He had not been able, morally, to keep them from crucifying him . . . his body! But he could prevent them from doing the greater evil of hurting his soul. He proved that a soul may be invulnerable . . . even on a cross.[9]

To dwell on blaming others for what has happened, however much it may have been their fault, is to do yourself a harm which others could not have done to you. Others can hurt you only if you help them to do so. Nothing can happen to you unless it happens in you; and in the inner citadel of your soul nothing can touch you unless you let it.[10]

5. *Doubt.*—Doubt concerning God's goodness, doubts concerning the motives of people who minister to them, doubts concerning their abilities to overcome the handicap which life has brought have constituted another battlefield on which many of our heroes and heroines have fought to victory.

C. S. Lewis summarized the doubt which has come often into the minds of people to whom sickness, sorrow, suffering, and handicap have come:

If God were good, he would wish to make His creatures perfectly happy, and if God were almighty, He would be able to do what He wished. But the creatures are not happy. Therefore, God lacks either goodness, or power, or both.[11]

Mr. Lewis pointed out splendidly in his book, however, what many of the fighters-against-doubt have found from a sane study of the universe. They have recognized that God has endowed men with freedom of choice—a freedom whose exercise has so often brought hurt to innocent people. They have taken knowledge of human failure and wickedness, and have come to the discovery that God never promised his children exemption from the hardships of life—promising them, rather, sufficient wisdom and power to turn the hardships into glorious victories. They have been much aware that even God's own Son, sinless and unoffending, was hurt by the perversities of human antagonism in the lives of the very people whom he sought to help. When these realities have dawned upon searching hearts, wonderful victories over the demon of doubt have been won.

6. *Anxiety.*—Several of the "high hurdlers" whose victories have been great inspirations to many have indicated that another of the downward tugs was the tendency to anxiety. Ned Shelton, mentioned in another chapter for his triumph over being bed-bound and blind, spoke of worry (of which anxiety is the inevitable result) in these discerning terms: "Worry is wonderful if it moves you to do things; corroding if it doesn't." [12]

Still another victor said to me: "Fruitless, nonconstructive worry led me to a constant state of anxiety; and, in short order, I added ulcers to my other problems and a fractious disposition to those nearest to me. In a sense of 'I've got to find help' I was searching the Bible and came across a sort of 'lifeline' thrown to me by the God to whom I had cried out for help. The lifeline was 1 Peter 5:7 (RSV), *'Cast all your anxieties on him, for he cares about you.'* Thereafter, I left the worrying to God and had more energy and initiative for creative thinking."

John Milton, distinguished English poet smitten with blindness, evidently had a victorious bout with the demon of anxiety. In his immortal Sonnet XIX, the sonnet on his blindness, he indicated initial anxiety that he had lost the light with which to use his chief talent. Listening eventually to the voice of patience, he came to the happy conclusion expressed in the final line of the sonnet: "They also serve who only stand and wait." The demon of anxiety, conquered by the heroes of our book, tries diligently to keep his intended victims from a willingness to stand and wait! [13]

7. *Impatience.*—When any well-and-strong person is touched suddenly by a handicap which may require months or years for recovery to a point of being able to do the things which earlier seemed as easy as breathing, or when a handi-

capped person must learn to adjust himself to circumstances of an entirely new pattern of living, the progress seems slow and interminable. The demon this person must fight and conquer at this point is the demon of impatience.

Miss Louise Luck of the "Surprised, but Not Overwhelmed" company of our brigade of the brave required the better part of a morning or afternoon to negotiate walking to the end of her residence block and back when she was first permitted braces and crutches. The resumption of household duties, which represented still another victory for her, was excruciatingly slow and tedious. She never "gave in" to impatience, and her victorious life has been a pattern for victory to thousands.

Brian Sternberg, another of the suddenly smitten company of the heroic, faced the incredibly slow process of learning to move one finger, then another, then another. Almost two years elapsed before he could write a short, simple note, a feat which he could have accomplished in five minutes prior to his impairment. He, too, routed the demon of impatience and continues to be a giant of inspiration and courage to all America.

8. *Stubbornness.*—An unwillingness to admit that the handicap has come to stay or a sense of resentment so deep that it paralyzes willingness to try to retrieve something from a broken life, or a false sense of pride in being too proud to accept the help of others in rebuilding life may be summed up well in the expression "demon of stubbornness." Several of our triumphant heroes have indicated that it became necessary early in their experiences with handicaps to face and vanquish this temptation to fight back at the circumstances. They recognized the futility of stubbornness and came to see that fruitful lives could be lived.

9. *Indiscreet counselors.*—In a misguided attempt to bring answers or comfort to people into whose lives handicaps have come, some friends and casual visitors presented still another "demon" which our victorious ones had to conquer: the demon of shallow, illogical, unthinking explanations of the coming of the handicap and the attitude with which to handle it. Although the heroes of this book did not always achieve a victory over this demon in the first encounter, they were, indeed, never down-and-out in its presence; and, with inspiring triumph of mind and heart, they beheaded this demon, too. In an explicit pattern of one victor's triumph, the reader will be greatly interested in Mrs. Iona Henry McLaughlin's experience, given later in this chapter.

10. *Despair.*—This vicious demon was normally a "late comer" in the experiences of our heroes—coming normally when a second or third handicap arrived before the first had been handled, or coming after slow or fruitless efforts to make adjustments to a restricted life. "Guess you'll ever make it. . . . Reckon you'd better stop trying. . . . Hadn't you best throw in the towel?" were the insidious suggestions rising in the minds of many of our most seriously handicapped heroes . . . often in the course of a lonely, fruitless day of trying, or in the stillness of sleepless nights which follow those fruitless days. Their victories over what might have been "black nights of despair" constitute a basis for special citation of these wonderful victors!

Pain: Demon or Angel?

Although many of the participants in the "Brigade of the Brave" had serious and protracted bouts with pain, suspecting it of demon qualities during its intensity, doubtless, they moved it to the "angel" classification in retrospect.

One who had suffered much for and with his children gave this insight:

Through suffering comes a vital discovery that we belong to Someone bigger than ourselves, the discovery of truth—that Nature is God's, and that Nature reveals God in some of his inevitables. . . . Our spiritual nature equips us with an instrument of unlimited power —the power to transform the meaning of suffering.[14]

Other veterans of the battle with pain have indicated that pain taught sympathy, patience, humility, appreciation of health, and a new dimension of gratitude for God's power, for friends, and for the effectiveness of prayer. These "happy warriors" have come to share, at least in part, the experience of Wordsworth's "Happy Warrior":

> . . . Doomed to go in company with Pain,
> And Fear, and Bloodshed, miserable train!
> Turns his necessity to glorious gain;
> In face of these doth exercise a power
> Which is our human nature's highest dower;
> Controls them and subdues, transmutes, bereaves
> Of their bad influence, and their good receives.

Many of our victors received indescribably great help from God's Word in their victorious handling of pain— notably from the book of Job and from the strong promises of God to be with his children to strengthen them. Also, many received strength from the helpful interpretations of writers whose books fell into their hands in hours of intense suffering. One passage which helped some of the heroes of our volume is this one:

We cannot be members of a society without being called to suffer through our relation to others. . . . The hardships of the pioneer and the discoverer, the risks of medical research, the loneliness and spiritual travail of the prophet which bring some new truth into the world, the agony of the martyr who witnesses to us, the wearisome nights and days of the nurse and the mother, the toil and disappointments of the teacher or pastor—all these and countless other forms of suffering find their sufficient explanation in the progress of the individual or the race.[15]

Nobody in our galaxy of victors over pain received a greater insight to pain or gained a more notable victory over it than did Mrs. Iona Henry. Her book, *Triumph over Tragedy,* is on my *must* list for any who are searching for victory through the morass of multiple difficulties and sorrows. In her book there is a chapter, "The Battle with Pain," and in that significant chapter there is this dramatic tribute to pain:

Pain? I know pain. You will know it, meet it, fight it, whoever you are. You must. It is a law of life that you just face pain. But this I have learned, in my fight with it: it is given to produce something better than tears and frustration. It produces love, sympathy and a brotherhood that is more spiritual than physical. There is deep purpose in pain; it opens our eyes to the methods of God with men. It brings out of the heart and mind the finest that God has put there. It sets deep calling unto deep, from heart to heart, in direct reply to the call of God.[16]

Therefore, we join our friends who are veterans and victors in the battle with pain in agreeing that *pain,* which often almost deceives one into shoving it into the "Demon" classification, actually can be an "Angel" in disguise to the discerning sufferer; and we join Mrs. Iona Henry McLaughlin in her suggestion of the appropriateness of a *Te Deum* to pain: *Angel,* not *Demon!*

Angels, for Sure!

In their valiant struggles to victory, the neither-down-nor-out heroes of our book have not fought the demons unaided. Although their allies in achieving victory have been largely inner qualities, these qualities have been fed and strengthened so often by family, friends, counselors, and forces made available by groups dedicated to assisting the handicapped. First, let us look into some of the qualities of mind and soul which aided them in their victories, observing those qualities in the heroic experiences of some of our brave victors.

Faith, giving rise to *hope,* gave many of the members of our "Brigade of the Brave" an emotional stability in their distresses; and this good basis of stability made possible their developing *determination, courage,* and *patience* with which to deal with their struggles for victory. The maturity which these qualities brought into their lives resulted in *unselfishness* in their demands of the families and friends who attended them and a genuine *gratitude* of heart for their allies in the struggle.

No individual in the decade of the sixties has demonstrated all of the foregoing qualities more illustriously than has *Mel Gimmaka.* According to United Press International's account of Mel's heroic victory, he had just completed high school with a basketball record of such outstanding caliber that he was being bidden by eleven colleges in the spring of 1962. He and three other youths in his West Coast community were returning from a church outing, and their car crashed into a bridge abutment, killing two of the youths, leaving Mel with a broken back and shattered left ankle. "You'll be lucky ever to walk again," was the consensus of medical opinion. "But medical experts picked the wrong guy for that kind of forecast," stated a news dispatch, "because today (1965) Gimmaka is a standout forward for the Seattle Pacific College Falcons, the defending West Coast NCAA college division champions."

His college coach said of Mel Gimmaka, when Mel was a twenty-one-year-old junior: "I don't know anyone who has more courage than he has. Mel is a fine Christian boy and a real leader. He is the inspirational spark that makes our team go."

In his first year in college, Mel wore a back brace and a cast from ankle to thigh. Though these impediments kept him from going out for the team, his faith, hope, determination, courage, and patience prompted him to hobble about the court hour after hour, practicing to keep his shooting eye keen and skilful. Later, aided by occasional pain pills, but primarily by dedicated courage, Mel participated in team play and led his team with a 14.3 average. Of Mel's triumph over handicaps of crippling and pain, the UPI reported the appraisal of his coach in these words: "It is evident that Gimmaka's injuries still cause him plenty of pain. But nobody ever hears about it from Mel. I've never heard him complain once. He just sets his jaw and goes on in spite of the pain. He just won't allow himself to be a cripple."

The same quality of courage, determination, and patience enabled *Ron Manka,* a Kansas lad, to become a football player with superlative skill in kickoffs, place-kicking, and field goals—despite the wooden leg with which he did his kicking. . . . And the same quantity of that quality of courage enabled *Donald Hamblen* to remain in the Marine Corps' reconnaissance parachute group after the loss of a leg in an earlier jump, hospital recovery, and adjustment to a mechanical leg. . . . And the same components of courage, determination, and patience enabled *Fred Rader* to become an outstanding athlete despite his blindness, and *Leah Russell* of Miami to become a successful member of a marching band despite her blindness. . . . And *Stephanie Smith* of New York to keep up her heroic battle against a rare blood disease for years, despite constant predictions of her death and repeated administrations of the last rites of her church.

Faith has been a tremendous ally to our victorious fighters with handicaps. *Clarence E. Power,* of the "Bed-bound, but Boundless" company in our parade, greeted the predictions of doctors that he could live only a short time with this prayer of faith:

Father I thank Thee for the gift of life. Strong, steady, deathless, it pulsates through me, bearing to every part of my body Thy assurance of love, wisdom, and wholeness.

I now surrender every personal doubt, fear, hard feeling, and shortcoming that would deny or retard the perfect flow of Thy life or love.

I am now open and receptive to Thee. I am putting on a new man, taking on the character of Christ. Father, I thank Thee for the gift of life.

For many years thereafter, Clarence Power not only lived, but improved steadily until he could sit up, use a typewriter, and carry on his "Sunshine Dispensation" throughout America.

The faith of Clarence Power and many others of our handicapped victors is reflected in the prayer of a writer whose insights gave some of our victors strength:

If it may be, lighten our burden, gladden our eyes, comfort our hearts, heal the sick body, and quiet the troubled mind. But, whatever may lie ahead, give us the assurance that thy friendliness enwraps us, that a wondrous purpose that cannot be defeated is being worked out in our lives, and that nothing can ever snatch us from thy loving care.[17]

Also these victors have shared the faith expressed by the same author in these lines:

Nothing that is allowed to happen has within itself the power finally and ultimately to defeat God. . . . So in the case of human suffering, God does not will it or desire it, but finally it will not defeat him in his plan for the individual sufferer—and he has such a plan for each of us. The fact that the suffering is allowed at all carries the guarantee that God, so far from being defeated by it finally, can weave it into a pattern as wonderful as one which left it out.[18]

Unselfishness of spirit has made many handicapped people literally "mountains of strength" to those who have surrounded them and who have been touched by the inspiration of their lives. So many of our handicapped heroes have been impelled by a compassionate desire to help others. Such has been the spirit of Dr. Sam Lawton of "Blind Who See" group in the parade of the victors. He has literally poured out his life to improve the happiness and usefulness of other blind people throughout America. Such was the spirit, too, of Clarence Power, who gave endless energy from the invalid couch to bring cheer and hope to other shut-ins.

The *forgiving spirit* has enabled many wounded, hurt, and handicapped people to overcome an inner bitterness which could have wrecked their happiness and usefulness. Such was the spirit of a man who was wrongly imprisoned in one of our state prisons, but who was freed later as a result of the testimony of the man who had actually committed the crime. The wrongly-imprisoned man forgave completely all those who had been responsible for his tragedy; and, so great was the victory in his life that he entered religious work as a vocation and is tremendously useful. . . . And such has been the source of victory of many others who have been physically handicapped by the carelessness or malice of others, or who have been bereft of members of their families by the failures of others, or who have been permanently hurt by the mistakes of others.

A resilient *sense of humor* and resultant *optimism* have served as lubricants to dispositions which, otherwise, might have worn thin, as "shock absorbers" which have kept the journey from jolting too sternly, as a fragrant essence with which they have made the whole world around them a happier place.

A man who had lost his sight in mid-life joked happily about his "being just out of sight but," he hoped, "not out of mind." A woman in the process of losing much of her hearing evoked smiles with her happy suggestion that she was the lucky one: she didn't have to hear the nerve-jangling clash and clatter of the world anymore. A man who had lost much of his business property in a tornado relaxed his anxious friends with the humorous observation, "I'll be the lucky one when income tax time comes around again!" A family of my acquaintance reports that the bedridden high school.son keeps the household "rocking with laughter" and that "he ought to be on TV." Still another family reported that it came to the bedside of a daughter, terminally ill of a malignancy, to relight its burned-out candles of faith and cheer from her happy and joyous spirit.

Angels Without Disguise!

Among the factors which have been "Angels of Aid" to our conquering heroes and heroines, there has been no larger factor than that of those who have "stood by" to help. Devoted members of the families of the handicapped have been willing to readjust their schedules and lives to give companionship and help. Friends have been willing to read to the blind, to write for the paralyzed, to run errands for the bed-and-chair-bound, to teach new skills to those who could practice former skills no longer, to give or raise money for equipment necessary to readjustment to a lifetime handicap, to love, to pray, to rejoice in every inch of progress.

Mothers of many of the handicapped have been skilled nurses without a day of nursing education; they have been discerning teachers without teaching certificates; they have been wise counselors without a semester hour of credit in psychology. Dads have worked at extra jobs to provide funds for expensive medical care or expensive equipment for their handicapped children. Sisters and brothers have readjusted their whole pattern of teen-age activity to assist the handicapped loved ones.

There have been many agencies which have developed programs to aid the handicapped in formal education, in vocational rehabilitation, and in obtaining equipment with which to adjust to worthwhile living. In their contributions these groups have been "angels" to multiple thousands of the victorious handicapped. Public education has been alert and helpful through special schools and classes; private foundations have demonstrated wisdom and compassion; governmental agencies have supplemented other groups in increasingly useful ways.

Queen of the Fray

The experiences of Mrs. Iona Henry, as presented in *Triumph over Tragedy*, combine the bouts with the demons and the help of the angels as splendidly as those of any person who has faced the fight and won the victory in our day.

Mrs. Henry had a long battle with *pain*, the culminating skirmish of which she won with sheer courage. She came *through the valley of despair* after the deaths of her daughter, husband, and son, and through her own experiences of being virtually broken to pieces. She learned and perfected *patience*, a victory which stood her in good stead during a long period of recovery and readjustments. Although the candles of *faith and hope* burned low in her early "bouts with the demons," the undimmed faith and encouragement of her devoted *friends* kept those candles burning until they flamed again into the full blast of *determination*.

Also, Mrs. Henry was victorious in her resistance of the "Job's comforters" who sought to give glib or shallow explanations of the tragedies which had come to her. In her splendid book, she delineates those rejected philosophies and suggestions:

1. There is a planned pattern; therefore, there is a purpose in all of this.
2. God loves you; so, he makes you suffer.
3. You are a substitute, suffering for other people.
4. Never mind. It's all right. Everything will be all right. Just don't worry about it.
5. It's just "Fate": when your time comes, it gets you.
6. It's just another case of the theory of good and evil: there is in this world a power for good (God) and a power for evil (Satan). You have been unfortunate in coming under the power of the evil one, who has just "let you have it" in this experience.
7. You must see a psychiatrist. . . .[19]

Her valiant fight against the inadequate explanations of her compounded tragedies continued until she spent long hours and days in unhurried conversation with her minister

father-in-law, to whom she dedicated her book and to whom
she paid this superb compliment:

TO DAD HENRY

WHO CAME TO MEET ME IN THE VALLEY

WITH GOD'S LANTERN IN HIS HAND

Dad Henry's philosophy was the first that really stood the
test, Mrs. Henry testified. She recognized his philosophy as
that of a mature mind—human understanding coupled with
the compassion of the God who made an orderly universe.
Because the philosophy reflects the way to victory achieved
by many of the "stars" of this volume, and because it could
be most helpful to a reader searching for a satisfying philosophy in tragedy, Dad Henry's counsel to his daughter-in-
law is summarized here:

. . . Look at the whole thing in the light of plain, ordinary common
sense, in the light of an orderly universe that runs under the reins of
law. When we break that law, either consciously or unconsciously, we
pay the penalty for breaking it. When we live in cooperation with the
law, even though we do not always understand it, we live well and
securely. . . . Some things happen in this world because we human
beings act like human beings, not because God makes them happen.
Just because your car got to that railroad crossing at the very moment
the train reached it doesn't mean that God planned it that way. God
makes certain laws. He gives men the know-how to create automobiles
and locomotives and to drive them at certain speeds. But it is *human*
planning and decision that bring a car and a locomotive to a certain
spot at a certain time. That's the working of the human will, and you
can't expect God to reach down out of high heaven to stop that car
or train, once their human drivers have set them in motion. That would
be to deny all the laws of movement and locomotion—*and it would
deny the right of the human being and the human will to make decisions, as well.*[20]

Mrs. Henry indicated that her beloved father-in-law used other illustrations to bring that important point into clear focus. One such illustration involved a man's fighting in a *man-made* war, confronted by *man-pulled triggers*: there- fore, if a man is killed in this man-made war by man-pulled triggers, it becomes illogical, if not ridiculous, to blame God for the soldier's death. Dad Henry's calm, compassionate reasoning concluded with these words: "No, it wasn't God's will or decision that the crash should happen. *It is not God's will that you suffer!*" [21]

Mrs. Henry's hungry search after a way to victory found the answer in the wise counsel of Dad Henry, and her re- action was expressed in these words: "It fell into my heart like rain on parched ground. How long I had waited to hear that! I had longed to believe it, but I had not thought through to it as he had. Not one in a million of us thinks it through; it's so much easier to say, 'Oh, it's just God's will.' We seem to know more about His will than He does, at times!"[22]

This remarkable woman, bereft of her entire family through tragedy and "graduated" from as vicious crucible of suffering as one can imagine, achieved what she called a "relaxed rapport" toward God and the circumstances of life, expressed beautifully in these sentences: "It is a mature attitude toward God, an alliance with a power greater than you are or ever can be, but a power that, nevertheless, re- spects you. It is an attitude of mutual respect and love. Of course God loves you; else, why would He have bothered to create you?" [23]

Mrs. Henry and the many other glorious victors over handicaps of every sort are irrefutable proofs that every child of God who fights the demons and accepts the aid of the angels *will find a way to complete victory over even tragic handicaps, and to joyous and fruitful adjustment to a life which has been altered, even completely, from its former pattern.* The ones who do not achieve victory have only themselves to blame; for, if they cooperate with the "angels," they, too, can join in the mighty chorus whose words were written by Paul, "I can do all things through Christ which strengtheneth me" (Phil. 4:13).

NOTES

1. Luther Robinson, *We Made Peace with Polio* (Nashville: Broadman Press, 1960), p. 43.

2. *Ibid.*, p. 165.

3. Theodore Adams, *Making the Most of What Life Brings* (New York: Harper & Row, 1957), pp. 88-89.

4. Iona Henry, *op. cit.*, pp. 50-51. (Now Dr. Iona Henry McLaughlin.)

5. Quoted in a daily column of "To Ann Landers."

6. Theodore Adams, *op. cit.*, p. 89.

7. Floyd Van Keuren, *The Open Door* (New York: Harper & Bros., 1942), p. 20.

8. *Ibid.*, p. 17.

9. *Ibid.*, p. 19.

10. *Ibid.*, p. 18.

11. C. S. Lewis, *The Problem of Pain* (New York: The Macmillan Co., 1943), p. 14.

12. Anne Morrow Lindbergh, *op. cit.*, p. 172.

13. Writings of John Milton, distinguished English poet.

14. H. Wheeler Robinson, *Suffering, Human and Divine* (New York: The Macmillan Co., 1939), p. 14.

15. *Ibid.*, p. 189.

16. Iona Henry, *op. cit.*, p. 49.

17. Leslie Weatherhead, *Salute to a Sufferer* (New York: Abingdon Press, 1962), p. 95.

18. *Ibid.*, p. 21.

19. Iona Henry, *op. cit.*, pp. 103-1C7.

20. *Ibid.*, pp. 101-110.

21. *Ibid.*, p. 111.

22. *Ibid.*

23. *Ibid.*, p. 117.

Closed Doors:

5 HINDRANCE OR HELP?

A very large book could be written, doubtless, concerning the experiences of people for whom doors of personal desire slammed shut . . . and locked. For some, the closed doors were permitted to become "curtains" on planning for the future, and they spent their days in regret that they didn't get what they wanted, blaming everybody and everything but their own attitudes for their frustrations. Others, however, while experiencing probable poignant regret at closed doors, walked on down life's hallway, finding open doors of opportunity, many of them actually grateful later that the doors which they had earlier wanted to enter did not open.

Long ago, someone pointed out that if only the first letter of the word *disappointment* were changed from *d* to *h*, the word would become *his-appointment*, the *his* referring to God. It is true beyond argument that some of the richest blessings to our world have come through the lives of people

81

who were directed by closed doors to other doors of service. For them, closed doors became guideposts and index fingers, not handicaps. Therefore, we may say that a closed door does not become a handicap unless the attitude of the person involved permits it so to become. Many who have not permitted closed doors to become handicaps, looking back over their years, have thanked God for closed doors—that their disappointments had become his-appointments. Let's meet some of these wonderful people.

A splendid young man graduated from college in 1907, hoping that, after teaching for a time, he could move on to a study of law, which was the only door of vocation he had ever really wanted to enter. Circumstances, involving the necessity of caring for younger members of his family, consumed his income, and there could be no savings. His alma mater invited him to return to teach in his chosen field. Graduate study became both desirable and necessary. Law school moved farther into the future, and the door finally closed.

By now, the fine young teacher had begun to feel that the door which God had opened in the teaching profession had rich challenges and definite gratifications. The opportunity to counsel, strengthen, and inspire young people became an increasing joy. He finished a doctorate in his field, taught with distinction; and, in the black night of the depression of the 1930's he heeded the call of the college to accept its presidency. He piloted the college through debt payments through war difficulties, through postwar problems of great growth; and, upon his retirement from the presidency, he left a college with its endowment tripled, with its buildings almost doubled in number, with its faculty strength and equipment increased and enriched, and with the student en rolment quadrupled. His name and influence will be immortal in the field of Christian education and in the life of that college. *But let's remember that he would never have written such a golden chapter if the door he preferred had not closed!*

A lovely, dedicated girl had chosen the door to religious work as the one which she wished to enter. She went to college to begin her preparation, but the death of her mother necessitated her withdrawal from college to pilot the home in which there were several younger children. These responsibilities lengthened into such time that it seemed next to impossible for her to complete college and seminary training. Circumstances beyond her control had closed the door which she wished so much to enter.

The door to marriage did open, however, and through the newly opened door she carried her dream of making a significant contribution to religious life. In the hearts of her children she deposited rich teachings from God's Word; she taught them the wisdom and joy of ascertaining and following God's will in their vocational choices; she gave an example of happy dedication which made her teachings all the more effective. To her joy, three of her sons have become ministers, one daughter was in religious work prior to her marriage, and another daughter lives abroad and exercises a splendid Christian influence in the land of her husband's citizenship. The experience of this wonderful woman can be summarized thus: *closed door, open door, life multiplied beyond her fondest dreams because she permitted dis-appointment to become his-appointment . . . she did not permit a closed door to become a handicap!*

Buddy had dreamed of college football all through his days of high school. He gained admittance to the college of his choice, played freshman football with success, and had returned for the presession training period as a prelude to varsity team participation. Before even the first game of the golden period of varsity performance for which he had dreamed, he became ill, and the verdict of the doctors slammed shut the door of his dreams with a resounding bang . . . polio! The best medical attention available in America ensued, but the damage was beyond the power of medical skill: his legs were completely paralyzed.

Grateful that his head and hands and heart were unaffected by the blow, Buddy strove with heroism to adjust himself to looking for a new door of opportunity, a door which he could enter in a wheelchair. Because he did not permit the frustration of his earlier dream to become a handicap, he found that door: he listened, studied, trained, and planned for a career in sportscasting. Furthermore, he disciplined his powers, routed his fears, and came to be able to wheel himself to his car, get into it without help, fold his chair, and to drive without assistance. Upon arrival at his destination he repeated his resourceful technique, and went to the elevator, arriving on his own at studios in his city. He was able, too, to attend all sports events. Today he is a highly valued staff member of one of America's outstanding radio and television stations and a widely-respected sportscaster, sports editor, and friend of the sports world.

A valiant young woman in her second year of study in dentistry experienced the tragic loss of both arms in an accident. One can hardly imagine a more heartbreaking loss to one who hoped for a career in dentistry. The door to the usual practice of that profession had shut and locked with apparent finality in the course of an afternoon's trip. A person of lesser courage might well have sat down on the door step of the closed door and have wept in despair, but this brave girl did not. With encouragement of professors, fellow students, and friends, she completed her course with the necessary modifications, and became a most useful visitor and lecturer in the field of dental hygiene. Later marriage to a college professor and the mothering of two splendid sons found her spirit in the same role of joyous triumph. *She has not permitted life to be abnormal for her, because she would not permit a closed door to become a handicap.*

Let's meet one more of the countless numbers in this brigade of bravery—the people who have found closed doors to be index fingers, who have found dis-appointment to be his-appointment, and who have come to careers of usefulness of great significance by entering the doors which did open.

From his earliest days of considering life investment, a young man in the Southwest had dreamed of entering medical missions. University days, medical college, internship, and marriage to a nurse had brought him now to the time of the long-looked-for entering of the door to service in medicine in missions supported by his denomination. In the process of the intense examinations which precede appointments to foreign missions, physical factors were discovered which made an appointment unwise. Despite the understandable ache of heart, he turned to search for an open door. This door opened in an opportunity to begin medical practice in an area in which the overwhelming portion of the population is of a foreign background in culture and language, an area in which the mission opportunity is tremendous. *Closed doors . . . valiant hearts . . . new doors . . . lives of infinite usefulness!*

Were time and space available, we could permit a concourse of similarly discerning people to pass in review. Some, to whom the door to marriage was shut, achieved victory over disappointment and self-pity, and moved along to lives of such service that thousands have received the warmth of their love. Others, to whom the doors of seeing and hearing have been closed, have "heard" with their hearts and have "seen" with their souls, bringing to their world rich blessings of literature, music, drama, and art. Still others, to whom the joy of children was denied, have become tremendous blessings to the children of other people through careers of service in which they have sublimated their parental desires so nobly. The names of these include men and women of all tongues, nations, and races; the nature of their closed doors includes the whole spectrum of human desire and endeavor; but regardless of the vast differences in location and background, these valiant ones have held these factors in common:

1. They have recognized that the greater wisdom of God and his vast personal love for individuals make necessary his closing doors if the doors chosen by his children are not life's highest and best plans for them. They know that, insofar as God's initiative in closing doors causes doors to close, there is a greater purpose for their lives than they had planned. They know that his justice implies that, if he takes the initiative to close a door, he will open another; they know that his power is so great, that he can assist the individual to overcoming disappointment, to finding the new door, and to achieving the maximum in entering it. In short, their faith in God has given stability to their thinking and planning when doors have shut to them.

2. They have recognized, too, that some doors close only temporarily and not permanently. Faith and patience enable them to wait until the permanence of the closing is revealed. These have found that, when a once-closed door reopens, they are much more ready to enter, and their happiness and conviction thereafter will be stronger.

3. These heroic ones have recognized that some doors which close are not God's closings, but are doors which are closed by circumstances initiated by carelessness, failures, or designs of other people. They know that all closings are not to be "blamed" on God. Their faith is adequate, moreover, to the realization that, even when circumstances outside his will have closed the doors, God's goodness and wisdom and power and presence are put at the disposal of the individual to help him to achieve success and happiness in a new relationship to life. They share Dr. Leslie Weatherhead's conviction that such circumstances are the "permissive will" of God, not his "intentional" will.[1]

4. They have followed Dr. Weatherhead to his final conviction, too: that God's "ultimate" will or purpose can be achieved in an individual's life, despite the fact that circumstances not of God's intention have necessitated an individual's seeking a new door for a door which has closed.

5. Emboldened and strengthened by such faith, these individuals have recognized the need for spiritual maturity in their reactions to closed doors and in their search for new doors—a maturity which has no place for self-pity, recriminations, bitterness, and settling for an unworthy living of a second-rate life.

AND YOU

What about your closed door—the one you now face or the one which may come tomorrow or far out in the tomorrows? If the closed door is a present reality, are you willing to admit that the heroes and heroines just presented have found the way of wisdom in dealing with closed doors; and are you willing to follow in that way? If the closed door is for you only a future possibility, are you willing to embrace now the faith which sustained them, to cultivate the courage necessary to implementing that faith with action if a door should close, to discipline yourself from now onward to a development of spiritual maturity? Remember: only you can determine whether or not your closed door shall become a handicap!

For the inspiration which it can bring now, and for the very real help which it can bring in the future, tuck away in your heart the following assurance, behind which stands all the power of God:

And we know that all things work together for good to them that love God, to them who are the called according to his purpose. . . . Nay, in all these things we are more than conquerors through him that loved us. For I am persuaded, that neither death, nor life, nor angels, nor principalities, nor powers, nor things present, nor things to come. Nor height, nor depth, nor any other creature, shall be able to separate us from the love of God, which is in Christ Jesus our Lord (Rom. 8:28, 37-39).

NOTES

1. Leslie Weatherhead, *The Will of God* (Nashville and New York: Abingdon-Cokesbury, 1944).

You Can Fail:
6 BUT YOU CAN'T QUIT!

Upon learning of my intention to prepare a book on victory over handicaps, a Virginia industrialist said with vigorous conviction, "Do a chapter on the topic, 'You can fail but you can't quit.'" He had in mind, doubtless, personnel experiences in his own industry in which individuals who had failed in early attempts had practically given up hope of succeeding. He expressed a strong conviction that failures do not need to become handicaps to future achievement and will not become handicaps unless the individual permits them to be.

This industrialist's experiences can be matched by many other instances from past and contemporary times. First, let us look into the nineteenth century for some inspiration from the lives of three men who failed, but who did not quit; and who, from the ashes of their failures, arose as wiser, finer men to achieve heights of success recognized by the world.

Some years ago, the *Reader's Digest* carried a stimulating article with the title, "He Could Take It."[1] The article tells of a young man of twenty-two years of age who had put his savings of seven years into a partnership in a store. Bankruptcy necessitated the closing of the store with the loss of every cent of the youth's investment. This failure, despite its bitter blow, did not keep him from trying again in another partnership. Because of the insobriety of his second partner, another business failure came and left a crushing debt.

Still not willing to quit, he obtained work as a surveyor, borrowing the money to purchase a horse and surveying instruments. Before he could begin the new work, however, creditors took the horse and instruments to apply on his debts. This third failure struck a hard blow, but not as hard as the subsequent tragic loss of his first love in death; for, as he himself said in later years, his heart was buried with her.

Four losses which would have broken the spirit of so many had touched him; and, though his spirit had not even thought of "giving up," his health failed, and a period of recuperation in the home of his parents was necessary. During this period of recovery, he probably assessed his losses, took a clear look at the assets of his spirit, and resolved to try again.

Turning from business, he tried for election to Congress; and, though he was elected and served, he was not returned to Congress by his constituents. Twice thereafter he attempted to win the senatorship in his state, but failed both times. Seven failures and a tragic loss, but still he had not thought to quit!

A short two years after his second loss of the contest for

the senate, a remarkable confluence of circumstances re-
warded his courage and faith: he was chosen by his party
as its presidential candidate and elected to the presidency
of the United States! He was Abraham Lincoln. Although
the whole world has eulogized him, the finest epitome of
this great man's career, in my judgment, is an application
of the Virginia industrialist's philosophy: HE FAILED, BUT HE
DIDN'T QUIT.

One can hardly imagine a defeat more distasteful, a
failure more bitter than that which General Robert E. Lee
acknowledged at Appomattox in 1865. The cause for which
he had fought with skill, spirit, and dignity rarely ever
found in such admirable quantities in one man had been
lost. Humiliation was heaped upon him from some sources,
particularly by the president's excluding him by name from
the general amnesty offered the South at the war's conclusion. Only Lee's application for pardon—an act designed to
humiliate him—brought the amnesty to him.

Free from bitterness as a result of the failure of the cause
to which he had been devoted, and free from recriminations
which blind many people whose failures are not primarily
of their own making, Lee turned to dedicate his total
strength to help in rebuilding a broken and exhausted South.
His brilliant success as an educator in the presidency of
Washington College (now Washington and Lee University)
gives another stirring proof that one can achieve tremendous
success after earlier defeats, *that is, if he doesn't quit!*

Storekeeper's Success

In the period following the War of 1861-1865, a young
man tried his hand at several ventures, tasting a succession
of failures. In a time-out, necessitated by the impact of

these reverses, he resolved to try again—this time with a small store in which people with but a nickel or dime to spend could find a large variety of articles from which to choose. His first such store opened with a stock of less than $500, but as a testimony of the faith and courage which keep a man from quitting after failure. The result of this man's unremitting courage is phenomenal: stores bearing his name now circle the globe; and, in its eighty-fourth year of operation, this company's sales stood at almost one and a quarter billion dollars.

More recent decades, including our own contemporary period, have seen glorious demonstrations of success which came to people who would not permit failures—often colossal ones—to persuade them to quit. Realizing that so many of the wisest and most useful people of this century have learned the way to success while conquering the crucible of defeat, the esteemed "Boss" Kettering of General Motors once said, "The main function of an educator is to teach young people how to fail successfully." Inspired by that thought, a college president prepared a tremendously helpful address for his students on the subject, "How to Fail Successfully."

Edison and other inventors of our time experienced many times of failure in their searches and efforts; yet, their keeping on after failure has brought to us the overwhelming majority of the comforts of this century. Some of our most widely-read-and-respected authors received a succession of rejection slips from the first articles they submitted. Some of our finest professional people are eminent successes in their current professions after failing in other work, but learning from their failures what were their weaknesses, their strengths, and their destinies. Many of our nation's most useful citizens were earlier failures in their patterns of living, but they learned from their failures the wisdom and pattern for successful personality control.

Why have many people either failed to try to do the jobs for which they feel suited and equipped, or why have they failed to try again after failure? From my own counseling experiences, decades of observation, many times of sharing with other counselors, and ceaseless reading I present this list of the main factors which have kept some individuals from trying and trying again:

1. *Fear.*—A paralyzing fear of initial failure or an immobilizing fear of a second failure has made of some people permanent failures—often in the sense of their not having achieved the vocational destinies for which they had the abilities. "I can't afford to fail," or "I'd just be humiliated to death if I should fail again," or "I'm afraid I don't really have the abilities" are some of their replies to "Why don't you try?"

   I tried through many hours and times of counseling to persuade a counselee to follow the dream he had in his heart, which dream he had come to discuss. He was earning a living in what he was doing, but he could not hush the voice in his soul which bade him give up a work in which he found no joy in order to try the work for which he had both ability and disposition. His self-defeating conclusion was this: "I could never face my family or friends if I didn't succeed, and I am afraid to take the risk."

2. *Doubt.*—Closely related to fear is the gnawing effect of doubt, which can chill the capacity of an individual to try again after failure. Dr. Norman Vincent Peale

tells the striking story of a gifted young surgeon who had failed in a significant early surgical operation and had been saved from tragedy and possible disgrace by the timely help of another surgeon. This experience so filled him with doubt concerning his capacity to do surgery again, that he came near to the point of "throwing in the towel" before trying again. Dr. Peale persuaded him to forget his past failure and to try again by leading him to believe these words: "I will forget the past forever. I will forget all my mistakes after I have derived knowledge from them. I will let God work through me in the great art of healing." The surgeon's doubts dissolved.[2]

3. *False pride.*—This is the sort of pride which keeps an individual from admitting failure, admitting that he was wrong, and prompts him to rationalization and buck-passing. This kind of pride, therefore, makes impossible an individual's learning wisdom from his failure. I dealt in his years of teaching and counseling with a significant number of students who were unwilling to assign their failures in studies or in conduct to their own laziness, lack of preparation, lack of integrity, or lack of cooperation. "It wasn't my fault. . . . If I had had half a chance. . . . I did the best I could, but the professor wasn't fair" and similar alibis were given. Fear of another failure *plus* false pride can add up to a quitter any day!

4. *Self-satisfaction.*—Some failures spring from the being satisfied with one's self to the degree of not trying for the maximum; or, having failed, the being content with a lesser degree of success rather than being willing to run the risk of another failure. This is the attitude

which a personnel director had in mind in saying, "When I hear one of our employees bragging repeatedly on his accomplishments, I begin to look for his successor"; and the attitude which a supervisor had in mind in saying to a teacher who had sought to defend her outmoded methods by contending that she had twenty-five years of experience in teaching that grade, "No, madam, you have had one year's experience twenty-five times!"

5. *Procrastination.*—The deceptive habit of knowing one can do it and intending to do it "one of these days" but deferring the doing is the explanation of the failures of many people of excellent abilities. In my own days of counseling on a college campus, I was obliged to say often to procrastinating students who "knew" they would do just fine when they were "up against it out in the world": *"Now* is just a minature of the future; and, if you become addicted to the habit of putting off what you can do and ought to do now, that habit will be your pattern in the future."

6. *Laziness.*—This habit is truly and tragically self-explanatory! So many have failed initially and refused to try again, not because of a lack of ability, but because of a lack of preparation and effort—both of which deficiencies grew up from sheer laziness of body or mind or both.

7. *Dishonesty.*—Some failures occur because individuals are not honest with the God who gave them their abilities and do not develop and use them; some are dishonest with themselves in not living up to the knowledge they have of what they could become; still others are dishonest, because they want to "ride to

success" on the efforts, influence, or money of other people. Some who fail are not willing to try again because they are not willing to pay in effort and sacrifice what they know real success will require.

8. *Antagonism.*—The oversensitivity toward other people's attitudes toward them or the undersensitivity to the feelings of other people cause bad relationships and frequent failures in the lives of many people. Dr. William C. Menninger, one of the world's best known and most highly respected psychiatrists, gave this discerning explanation of the failure of many who have the ability for success: "The difference between success and failure depends on knowing how to get along with other people. . . . About 80 per cent of the people fired from their jobs are dismissed because they don't know how to get along with people they work with or for."[3] It follows that an individual who is unwilling to adjust his thinking, feelings, and actions to working with other people submits himself to continuing failure.

The Other Side of the Coin

To conclude our consideration of failing-but-not quitting, let's look at the opposites of the eight foregoing failure factors:

1. *Faith* (instead of fear).—This involves faith in God, faith in oneself, faith to believe that if one does his best, God will do the rest. This faith in God makes it easy and very real for the individual to believe that God has given to him the abilities which he needs to accomplish the vocational purpose which God has for his life, to believe that God will fulfil his promises to

accompany and assist the individual (Isa. 41:10, 13), to believe that God will supply all of his needs (Phil. 4:19); and that, therefore, he can do all that God meant him to do (4:13).

2. *Belief* (instead of doubt.)—Confident belief enables an individual to feel that, regardless of the difficulties of preparation and performance, he *can* accomplish the purpose of his life. This sort of belief led a young man into medicine, despite earlier fears and doubts concerning a personal weakness and deep inhibition concerning one area of medical practice. When belief displaced doubt, he went through medical college with honors and has become an outstanding physician.

3. *Humility* (instead of false pride).—This spirit enables the one who has failed to admit his failure, to accept the blame for it, and to seek to know the reasons in order to try again. It is the sort of spirit which the distinguished Dr. Louis Evans, nationally known Presbyterian minister, had in mind saying that the six bravest, hardest words in our language are these: "I was wrong: I am sorry." Only humility enables one to say those words, right the wrong, and try again!

4. *Ceaseless Ambition* (instead of self-satisfaction).—This trait is, in large part, the explanation of Abraham Lincoln's willingness to keep trying after a succession of failures. This spirit explains, too, the eager willingness of the apostle Peter to keep trying after several notable failures. This same spirit impelled Paul to keep striving to the end of his life, despite many frustrations and obstructions. Ceaseless ambition implies that, after having lost and admitted failure in a humble, graceful spirit, the individual tries again.

Also, Author Mildred Seydell voices this wise insight: "It is not humanly possible to live without failing. But it is possible to fail and begin again. Match every fall with a rise—the reward will be rich."[4]

5. *Promptness* (instead of procrastination).—Many people of lesser abilities have won more success than some of larger abilities; they were there, on time, ready to go. Their more talented contemporaries "had it" but were not there to deliver. Admiral Nelson, of British Naval fame, is reported to have explained his success by saying that he had always been fifteen minutes ahead of time! The failure who means to try again "one of these days when things are more favorable" will be a quitter inevitably.

6. *Industry* (instead of laziness).—Many people, less talented than others, have succeeded admirably through hard work. The Bible tells of a wonderful feat of construction because the people "had a mind to work." Life all about us reveals successes by "average" individuals because they "had a mind to work."

7. *Integrity* (instead of dishonesty).—There are some wonderful ones among us whose honesty of soul demands that they give their best to preparation and performance; and, if some of these fail in early attempts, they try again with honest attempts to correct the causes of their failures. These are the ones who "provide all things honest in the sight of God," and who "walk honestly as in the day." These are the ones who could not "live with themselves" if, having failed, they did not honestly try again.

8. *Adjustment* (instead of antagonism).—A wonderful book of true-to-life stories could be written concerning

people who, having failed in one working relationship, realized that the cause of their failure was poor adjustment to the situation or to other people, who corrected the "inner maladjustment" and tried again—in the same work and with tremendous success.

Some Failures in Perspective

Some failures after repeated tryings-again are not actually failures, looked at from a perspective of the ages. Some of the finest artists of the past have presented pictures which the world rejected and for which these artists were paid but pittances; yet, some of those same pictures now are acclaimed as immortal masterpieces. Some works of literature and music were received without appreciation and with little or no compensation at the time of their completion, but they are now declared to be the finest representatives of their types extant. And we remember with hearts touched deeply that, on a Friday so long ago, Christ on a cross was declared to be a failure after three years of trying and trying again; but we realize, too, with hearts touched with joy, that his influence in our world is the greatest force for uplift in existence, and that people of all walks and abilities rejoice to give him honor.

While reminding those who are wrestling with the problem of failure and trying again *not* to classify their failures in this category as an escape mechanism or as a rationalization technique, it is only fair to recognize that there have been some people through the ages whose very best efforts seemed crowned with final failure, but whose "failures" have become tremendous blessings to succeeding generations. These people had *been* their best, had *tried* best, had *given* themselves completely to their missions; there was no more they could do, save waiting for history to vindicate their lives.

In a number of instances, your author has seen a poem whose authorship is generally hidden in a "Selected" or "Anonymous" citation, a poem which some readers may wish to tuck away in their hearts:

Don't Quit

It is easy to quit when you're losing
And nobody else seems to care. . . .
The side roads of life are all littered
With folks who gave up in despair

If a cripple can thank God for crutches,
And a blind man can smile in night's pit,
When the world gets you down, count your
blessings,
And whatever you do, never quit!

NOTES

1. Arno B. Reincke, "He Could Take It," *Reader's Digest*, January, 1939. Reprinted in issue of February, 1963, pp. 140-142.

2. Dr. Norman Vincent Peale, "Look Ahead with Anticipation," Foundation for Christian Living, Pawling, N.Y.

3. Dr. William C. Menninger, "Why Men Fail," *This Week Magazine*, March 27, 1955, p. 7. Copyrighted.

4. Mildred Seydell, *Chins Up* (New York: Grossett and Dunlap, 1939), p. 22. Used by permission.

Mistakes in the Past:
7 NO ALBATROSS!

You remember the *Rime of the Ancient Mariner,* doubtless, and will recall that the central figure of the story wore about his neck the dead body of an albatross. He was wearing this bird of the sea as penalty and reminder of the wrong he had done in killing the bird which had been an omen of good fortune to the ship's crew.

That gripping episode of literature has brought to mind often this analogy: Some people who have made grave mistakes in the past continue to wear those mistakes in their hearts through the years, grieving over irreparable errors, not forgiving themselves, finding it difficult to believe that God and many of their fellowmen have forgiven them.

Despite the reluctance or unwillingness of some people to forgive or to forget, God's Word makes clear the Heavenly Father's willingness and readiness to *forgive* us, to *remove* our transgressions from us as far as the East is from the West, and to *remember* these trespasses *against us no more.*

During his earthly ministry, Christ forgave such transgressors as the woman caught in adultery, dishonest Zacchaeus, the social outcast at the Well of Sychar; and on the cross he forgave even his revilers. In the Acts 9 conversation involving Paul's dreadful wrongs toward Christianity, forgiveness is clearly implied. *All* of these and many like them were forgiven, and some of them were used significantly in Christian ministries thereafter.

It is my fervent hope that any readers who have continued up to now to "carry an albatross" of unremitting regret for some mistakes in the past will find in the lives of people mentioned here the encouragement to fling to the winds the haunting shadow of past errors; and, having learned whatever those mistakes of yesteryears can teach, to move forward to lives of significant usefulness and happiness. Mistakes of the past will become no more of a handicap than we permit them to become. So, regardless of the "size" of your mistake in the past—simple or serious, trite or tragic, only self-injuring or hurtful to others—please do move forward in these pages in the knowledge that you, too, can turn past mistakes from being a factor of doom into being a help in achieving the destiny of your life.

It is difficult, if not actually dangerous, to "divide" mistakes into categories or listings; but, for the sake of some method of procedure, the following listings have been chosen. Quite naturally, there are overlappings in the listings; therefore, the reader will not regard the suggested divisions as necessarily completely accurate and, most surely not authoritative!

Mistakes in Effort and Progress

There are some people who seem to be unable to recogniz

that mistakes are an inevitable part of the lives of people who are finite in wisdom; therefore, they are crushed by any mistake made in their efforts. Often people are so afraid of making mistakes, that they are practically paralyzed in initiative and, therefore, fail to accomplish life's greatest adventures and thrills.

It is a fact of human experience, proved by the biographies of many people, that impressive later successes grew out of what those people had learned from mistakes made earlier in their lives. A most excellent article by Beth Day appeared in the December, 1965, issue of *Guideposts* magazine with this remarkable title done in red ink in the center of the page: "You have a right to your misstakes!" The misspelled word "misstakes" was marked out by a line drawn through it and the proper word "mistakes" set above it.

In that article, the author relates several impressive instances of people who went forward despite their mistakes, but learning something helpful from each one of them. She tells of the experiences of Admiral Robert E. Peary in making unsuccessful Artic expeditions, recording after each trip his mistakes, making new plans with the wisdom the mistakes had brought, and eventually making the great discovery of the North Pole.

Beth Day's article concludes with this remarkable observation concerning Winston Churchill:

On the international political scene, young Winston Churchill made so many outrageous errors that he was damned by the press for his "lack of discretion and judgment"—an indictment which, if he had allowed it to curtail his activities, would have robbed the Allies of a magnificent leader during the darkest years of World War II.

That excellent article concludes with a quotation from

Emerson, which quotation could be followed with great profit by any reader who has been "haunted" by mistakes in the past in his efforts to do his work or to go forward in progress—or who, perhaps, has become almost resigned to a lesser level of achievement than his abilities justify, rather than to risk the possibility of other mistakes:

Finish each day and be done with it. You have done what you could. Some blunders and absurdities no doubt crept in; forget them as soon as you can. Tomorrow is a new day; begin it well and serenely, and with too high a spirit to be cumbered with your old nonsense.

What can you learn from mistakes in your work or personal relationships to give you wisdom and strength for those same areas in your tomorrow?

Mistakes of Judgment

Mistakes of this kind normally are not intended and do not involve a conscious violation of rules or laws. Individuals find it necesary to arrive at decisions, to make choices, to react to situations, to offer appraisals, to render verdicts. Such decisions are usually made in the light of one's present knowledge or in the light of evidences as seen by the individual; and many have been the mistakes made because of inadequate knowledge, or of knowledge not wisely applied, or of insufficient evidence at hand! If, however, the individual's knowledge is increased through the mistake, if he learns to apply his knowledge more wisely, and if he demands more evidence before future decisions, his mistakes have been an excellent teacher, and he may come to be a person of astuteness.

Sir Walter Scott made an error of judgment in the choice of a publishing partner. This mistake brought financial catastrophe; yet, because of the mistake, Sir Walter gave to the world a very rich twofold legacy: (1) the example of a man of honor who would not dishonor debts even if legally excused, and (2) a wealth of literature which has warmed the hearts of millions of readers and challenged the best on the part of other writers. A businessman made an error of judgment and lost his fortune; yet, from the experience he learned so much of wisdom and came to such a magnifiicent sense of values of life itself, that hundreds of people seek his counsel yearly.

A Sunday School teacher who had declared a junior boy in her department to be incorrigible and beyond all hope of rehabilitation, wept in remorse later in learning that another teacher had "found the key" to the boy's heart and had discovered him to be a "diamond in the rough." This error of judgment led the first teacher to a reexamination of her whole philosophy and of her bases for appraising youngsters. So much has she learned from her earlier error of judgment that she is now a much loved worker with "problem children" and one of the nation's most effective advocates of the "tender, loving, understanding approach" in child care.

A college president committed a serious error of judgment in "reading out of the book of success" a student who was withdrawing from school for reasons which the president misinterpreted. The president's inadequate knowledge of the boy's reasons and his insufficient knowledge of the student's courage and persistence led to this error of judgment. Be it said to the credit of the college president, however, he later realized his error of judgment, invited that former student (at the time, a high government official) to deliver a commencement address, and to serve on his Board of

Regents. More than that, the president became infinitely more careful and successful in his appraisal of students with problems.

One of the most notable mistakes of judgment in recent years occurred in the actions of a professional athlete. He was suspended by the commissioner of that sport for a year. In a refreshing demonstration of sportsmanship, he admitted his mistakes, apologized to those whom he had disappointed, and expressed splendid intention of living up to the highest codes in the future. Upon his return to the professional sport which he loved so much, he demonstrated in tangible ways that he had benefited from his mistake of judgment, and all America watches his splendid performances with a new note of admiration.

Mistakes of Indiscretion

A university student from an excellent family background, normal church life, and happy associations had been asked by the university not to return in the fall. Although he honestly knew better than to commit the act of indiscretion for which he was being punished, "so many others were doing it; and, after all, it didn't seem nearly as indiscreet as a lot of other things students were doing!"

Now that the blow of expulsion had come, he was appalled, crushed, and wondering what he should do. Fortunately, he was quick to admit the mistake and to take a good, long look at himself—his strengths, his weaknesses, his needs for maturity of judgment and courage. Then, confiding his whole story to officials of another university, he asked to be accepted on probation. He gave such wonderful evidence of his having learned and grown since the indiscretion of his earlier experience, that he graduated with the deep admiration of a whole institution, and went forward into a life of great usefulness.

Another student, invited by his college to withdraw because of indiscreet conduct, took a long time-out at home. He reviewed his whole life, admitting weaknesses and relating those to his present plight. He came to a very clear concept of the strengths which he needed to cultivate. For the first time, he related himself soberly and unselfishly to life in the matter of vocation. No maker-of-mistakes has ever come through with greater wisdom than did this young man! The significance of his profiting from mistakes is indicated by the rather glorious fact that he returned as college minister to the same college six years later!

A man, successful in business, but a failure at living, was widely known for his indiscreet conduct. In a tremendous religious experience, he viewed with clarity and amazement the vastness of his mistakes in living. Although keenly penitent and fully remorseful, he did not permit the mistakes of indiscretion to become an albatross about his neck. Believing God's promises of forgiveness, he looked at his past only to derive lessons for strength in the future, and he marched forward into a life which has become widely useful throughout America. He has become a living, inspiring example to thousands who, too, have made mistakes of indiscretion, for he points them to the way of victory and acquaints them with the power to walk in that way.

Mistakes of Illegality

Doubtless, the greatest challenge faced by people who have made mistakes in the past is faced by those whose mistakes have brought public censure and, in many instances, court sentences and imprisonment. Yet the victories of many of this group in refusing to let these grave mistakes doom their future constitute a brilliant proof that past mistakes do not have to be handicaps to future usefulness and happiness. It will be helpful to those with similar problems from the past to meet some of these courageous ones and to know a bit about the factors which helped them to turn a tragic experience of the past into strength for themselves and others. They constitute an unusual group portrait.

There, on the left in this group picture, stands a man who was "on his way up" to the highest level of officialdom in the financial institution with which he was connected—until the audits revealed embezzlement! A term in a federal institution followed, during which he underwent a complete transformation within: dishonesty, vanity, selfishness went out; integrity, humility, hunger to serve mankind came in. At this writing, he is taking special training which will make possible his becoming a lifetime counselor and helper to others who have made mistakes.

To his left in the portrait stands one who was awarded the Purple Heart for his heroism in war, but who was later sent to prison for an act of fraud. Upon his being paroled a few months later, to quote his own words, he was "walking a new road," because he had "found a new life in prison." The new road led to a seminary for theological study and to a life of usefulness in the future. The judge who presided at the time of his parole expressed a sentiment which can give hope for others who, having made grave mistakes, have "found a new life" and have learned from those mistakes: "I think that maybe this is one of those storybook tales where someone has really surmounted a real heavy burden and shows intestinal fortitude to come through."[1]

Reading from the left, the third man in this group portrait

is one concerning whom a *Reader's Digest* article said in headline: "He Turned Disaster into Triumph."[2] Following several times of back surgery and recurring periods of near-interminable pain, he moved into heavy use of narcotics; and, despite the fact that he was actually on the road to victory, the records found by the law-enforcement agencies told an irrefutable story of addiction. From a successful teaching career he went to prison and to a time of deep introspection, followed by uplook and outlook. He organized a school for the youngsters in prison, conducted it with skill and compassion; and, upon his release from prison, he was employed to act as a teacher-director of the prison school which, doubtless, is already becoming the pattern for many similar schools throughout the prison systems of our nation.

The fourth man in the picture is now a highly successful physician and surgeon in the field of opthalmology, bringing eye healing and restoration to a large number of people every year. But he didn't start out to be a doctor: he was on his way to a life of crime. In burglarizing the office of a prominent businessman one night, he was surprised by the businessman himself, who had returned to his office for some papers. A fight ensued, in which the youngster injured the businessman gravely, including particularly serious eye injuries. A court scene and a sentence followed; but, thanks to the compassion of the businessman who had suffered the grave injuries, but who had learned of the youngster's tragic background prior to the episode of burglary and injury, the wrongdoer was treated sympathetically. Thanks to the wrongdoer's response to the kindness and counsel of his benefactor, the young might-have-been criminal changed his whole concept of life. He made a vocational decision for medicine and the specialization upon diseases of the eye because of the experience in which he had inflicted injury earlier upon his benefactor. What might have been a mistake which doomed has become a factor in a bright destiny.

If the range of the camera which made the foregoing portrait were wider, many others would appear in the group portrait: they made mistakes for which society decreed punishment; in months or years of imprisonment they experienced the urge for self-examination and correction of weaknesses; many of them actually found new and wonderful ways of creative self-expression with which they have later blessed their world; they have emerged from prison walls to become some of society's best benefactors.

What are the factors which helped these makers-of-tragic-mistakes to turn those mistakes into mirrors and teachers, which helped them to reenter a free world in such state of mind and heart that their mistakes did not become a version of the Ancient Mariner's albatross? Their own testimonies can bring helpful answers. Let's hear some of those answers.

1. *They cleared up their thinking and corrected their attitudes.*

One businessman expressed it thus in looking back over his prison experiences: "When I first entered prison, I was bitter, depressed. I felt small and unimportant."

A news writer described this man's initial attitude in prison thus: "His self-image was shattered. He was shocked. He felt dead. He was almost agnostic."

The businessman himself described the process of the clearing up of his thinking and the correction of his attitudes in these words: "Mostly because there was nothing else to do, I began to read and think."[3]

Another man, writing from his prison cell, gave evidence

that his self-examination, clear thinking, and frank admission of his wrongs made possible his admitting that he had stolen for no reason that even he could endorse, that he had wronged the best friend that he ever had, that he and he alone was responsible for this present state. Still another man in prison, having cleared up his thinking and corrected his attitudes, admitted freely to a minister-counselor that he had made a mistake for which there was no justification. In short, these men recognized that wrong thinking and wrong attitudes had brought them to their present misfortunes, and that only right thinking and right attitudes could help them to become different men.

2. *Having corrected their attitudes, they began to search for a better pattern of living.*

"I felt the need for something better than the bad times before," said one man, just out of prison and on his way to preparation for a useful life. Sometimes, this coming to want a better pattern for living seriously enough to search for it has come largely from self-examination, thought, and prayer. At other times, those processes have been supplemented with readings and study in prison libraries. In many instances, the search for a better pattern of living has begun from the help of counselors—chaplains, visiting ministers, or friends who write. But, regardless of how the desire and search began, it was a large factor in their rehabilitation.

3. *With attitudes corrected, and with search for new patterns of living begun, they began to prepare for a new life in freedom.*

Some began to study informally under the guidance of prison educational provisions; some began to complete education programs which they had dropped in earlier years; and in this group there are those who have completed high school courses and as much as a year of correspondence credit in colleges. Others have found new ways for the use of their abilities and new avenues for self-expression, now using them constructively.

In one prison, self-expression through art is encouraged, and a yearly exhibition of the pictures done by the prisoners is held. In one such exhibition, the men received over $12,000 for the pictures which were on sale. Some of these men will pursue art as careers when freedom comes. Who knows: one or more of these men may give to our world masterpieces with the abilities discovered or redirected as they prepared for new life beyond prison walls?

From some of our state prisons groups of prisoners go frequently in company with the superintendents to speak to high school assemblies. They remind the students that they were once just like their listeners: they had dates, made class trips, had all the usual fun of high school students, and wouldn't have believed it if someone had told them that they would be prisoners someday; but that bad habits and a general misdirection of their abilities brought them to their present state. They speak clearly, effectively, giving living demonstrations of the end result of carelessness, drinking, speeding, and malicious mischief. In addition to contributing a monumental character-strengthening to high school audiences, these men are having an experience of directing their abilities and influence in creative, constructive directions; therefore, they will be admirably suited for constructive lives beyond prison walls.

Sydney J. Harris, widely-read columnist, expressed the miracle of redirection in this effective paragraph:

Some of our worst elements are to be found in prison—and some of the potentially best, as well. The qualities that go into the making of a talented criminal are often the same qualities that would make a resourceful leader in the arts and professions: independence, resourcefulness, and a craving for creative, non-routine activity.[4]

4. A fourth factor in the turning of their mistakes from handicaps to progress factors was *their willingness to accept the help available to mistake-makers who want to live victoriously in the future.*

Despite the unforgiving and unforgetting attitude of a portion of our society, there is wonderful help available in the battle to keep past mistakes from becoming handicaps. Some of these helps are available to individuals while still in prison; other helps literally "wait at the prison gates" to assist individuals who are willing to accept help.

There are *programs* within the prison itself to enable an individual to begin the process of redirection of his life. Programs of study, self-expression in creative projects, and counseling for the present and future are available in almost all penal institutions. They are voluntary, however, and a man must want these helps and ask for them.

There are *people* who stand ready to assist mistake-makers to turn their mistakes from factors of doom to factors of destiny; counselors, ministers, dedicated Christians, lawyers, lay people who are filled with the spirit of Christ, and some personal friends who have the added motivation of personal ties in assisting mistake-makers.

There are *organizations* and *foundations.* Hope Enterprises, Inc., and the Robert Lindner Foundation in one of our Eastern cities are two representatives of many foundations which exist to help people who have the could-be handicap of mistakes of illegality to consider. The latter of the two organizations just mentioned makes awards in art, literature, and music to creative prisoners.

5. There is the *incomparable help to be had from the exercise of the privileges of the Christian faith: the reading and study of God's Word, the faith to apply it to one's needs, the resultful exercise of the communion of prayer, and the vital companionship possible with Christ himself.*

Many former prisoners have testified that they found that *reason* alone was inadequate to explain what they had done in the past and what they needed to do in the future; but that, when they searched God's Word, they found new thoughts, they discovered passages which gave them hope, they believed what they had read, they took new hope, they prayed, and new life began. One near-agnostic said, "I found that only God's Word and Christian faith gave all the answers I needed concerning my past and all the guidance I needed for my future." One of the Bible passages which brought his past and future into focus and pointed the way to victory for him was 2 Chronicles 15:2: "The Lord *is* with you, while ye be with him; and if ye seek him, he will be found of you; but if ye forsake him, he will forsake you."

Others have reported that they came to an entirely new and vital concept of fellowship with Christ in realizing that in Matthew 25:36 he equated personal ministry to himself with ministering to the needs of people in prison: "I was in prison, and ye came unto me." They felt a thrill in realizing that Christ, whose spirit visited Peter, Paul, and others in jail, cared enough for them to make his presence felt in their hearts, too. And the empowering companionship of Christ has enabled many of them to face the future with the faith and courage of Philippians 4:13.

Build a Bonfire

How long has it been since you were present for a bonfire —at a retreat, or an evening picnic, or at a pep rally prior to the game of the year? Remember the thrill of your heart at the leaping flames of the bonfire and what the significance of the occasion meant to you? Generally speaking, the bonfire indicated a climax to an experience or the high point of preparation for a great effort in the immediate future.

Why not build yourself a figurative bonfire now, tossing into the flames the memory of the mistakes of the past— insofar as the memory has been a deterrent to progress, usefulness, and happiness? And, as the flames of forgiveness and forgetting attend to those haunting mistakes, rejoice in the bright light of the lessons you have learned, commit your life anew to the wisdom and power of God, and turn away from the bonfire with the zest for victory in your soul. The Ancient Mariner didn't wear that albatross forever, and neither should you!

NOTES

1. Associated Press reports, July 19, 1960.
2. Martin Abramson, in *Reader's Digest*, December, 1960.
3. Associated Press reports, *Alabama Journal*, July 19, 1960.
4. Sydney J. Harris, "Jailed Genius," *Nashville Banner*, July 13, 1962. Reprinted by permission of Sydney J. Harris and Publishers' Newspaper Syndicate.

The Night of Sorrow:
8 THIS, TOO, SHALL PASS

"God had no right to take my husband away, sobbed a woman just bereft of her devoted mate. . . . An she lived out her life in a bitterness born of her own illogica attitude.

"I have nothing now to live for," wept another at th accidental death of her only child. . . . And, though sh *existed* physically thereafter, she did not really live.

"All I have lived for died with my son," grieved a fathe: "All of me that really counts was buried with my husband, explained a sorrow-smitten widow. These, too, had made c sorrow a handicap which did not have to be.

But there are others into whose lives great sorrows came who conquered their black nights of grief; and, in th remarkable partnership with God's power, they have turne their sorrows into songs—songs which have serenaded th midnight hours in the lives of other grief-stricken peopl with music of faith and courage. Their examples have becom

116

bright stars of promise and cheer in the darkened skies of some whose grief had brought them to the verge of the valley of despair.

In the process of learning how to handle sorrow, lest it become a handicap to happiness and progress, the triumphant ones mentioned in the foregoing paragraph have recognized that sorrow is the common lot of all mankind: that it is not unusual, that it is as logical as birth, that it must be taken into life and made a part of life, that no amount of railing and running can remove its reality from life. They share the sentiment of a poetess who knew the taste of sorrow:

> "There is no God," the foolish saith,
> But none "There is no sorrow."
> And Nature, oft in bitter need,
> The cry of Faith will borrow.
>
> Eyes which the preacher could not school
> By wayside graves are raised—
> And lips cry, "God be pitiful."
> Which never said, "God be praised."
>
> Elizabeth Barrett Browning

Realizing the inevitability and normalcy of sorrow, these triumphant ones have developed resources for meeting and handling grief in advance of its actual arrival. They have felt that since people take out insurance against the possibility of sickness, hospitalization, and loss of property—just to be prepared in case such losses should come, they are logical in "taking out spiritual insurance" against the day in which sorrow may come. In the Channel Press book *You and Your Grief* (1961) Edgar Jackson has listed some of the resources for meeting grief. Some of the resources, followed by any comments, are:

1. *"Belief in the goodness of God, who has taken your loved one unto himself . . . You are releasing the loved one to his care."*

In a crisp, cool, star-lit predawn hour, I stood outside the cottage to which a beloved member of my family was returning from a seventy-two-hour vigil at the bedside of her little son, a vigil which had ended as the lad's spirit took flight to the presence of God. This was the third in a series of sorrowful events and seemed to be the heaviest of them all, for he was her bright star of hope for the years ahead. Very really, the favorite melody had been torn suddenly from the repertoire of her heart; the last little star in her firmament of hope had twinkled and gone out. Had God treated her unkindly, and should she storm at heaven's gates in her hour of vast loneliness?

As I sought to say words which might assuage the grief of her tremendous loss, I was thrilled to hear this heroic woman say: "I know what you are trying to say; and, though I am so grateful to you, let me make haste to say that you do not need to worry about me. I know so much about the goodness of God, about his wisdom which sees far into the future and sometimes permits a lesser sorrow to forestall a greater one. Something could have happened to my precious little son in the years ahead which could have been so much worse than death. Now I know that he is very safe in the arms of God, and all that is good and fine in him will surely keep growing with nothing of earth's sin to hurt him. So, trusting God and knowing of his love and care, I would not call my little son back to life if I could." That is *belief in the goodness of God.*

One of the most triumphant books of recent years is, *We Made Peace with Polio*. The author of that book had rushed one daughter to a distant hospital and had discovered that bulbar polio had smitten her. While keeping vigil in the hospital, he had been called to rush back to his community because of the mysterious illness of another daughter. This second daughter died of a difficult-to-diagnose form of polio before the night was gone.

He was now faced with the task of going to his wife, still stunned and exhausted by this sudden blow to both of her daughters, to tell her of the latest sorrow. He stood outside the residence in which his wife was sleeping, looking at the dawn, and meditating before going in to break the news of the daughter's death, and these were the words he recorded in his book:

How I could feel, in moments of sorrow, that all things are good and beautiful, I cannot explain. But I did feel that even then sorrow must have some end in itself: to ennoble, enrich, and inspire after the terrible journey of anxiety and fear. Perhaps I learned then what others had known before: that when the spirit is alone and humbled, it may then be given peace and some strength greater than itself.[1]

His meditations concerning the wisdom and goodness of God continue:

I thought of Anita (the deceased daughter) also . . . of all that might have happened to her had she lived to be a badly crippled girl. Anita might never have been happy in a badly crippled body. . . . No, we wouldn't call her back if we could, not in a body badly broken and crippled . . . by polio.

2. *"Belief in eternal life"* is Edgar Jackson's second suggested resource for meeting grief.

I stood with a large group of friends one late afternoon in a cemetery in which the body of a distinguished educator was being committed to the grave. The widow of the deceased man lifted her face with a beautiful look of faith and peace as the casket was being lowered, and her glasses caught up the orange glow of the setting sun, giving her face a graphic radiance. There seemed to be written into her face the confidence that, just as the sun was setting now with promise of rising on the morrow, her husband's body was being planted in the earth now with the promise of rising on some distant tomorrow. . . . That, though he was absent from physical sight, he did live on as really as ever . . . That in the assurance, too, that she would live on past death, she would see him again.

In later conversation with this remarkable woman, I discovered that those were, indeed, her convictions. Her belief in eternal life had made possible her believing that her separation from him was only temporary, and the confident joy of eventual reunion made possible her turning her sorrow into a song of faith and expectations. She felt, too, that since life in a vastly larger way was continuing for her husband, life in abundant service must continue for her too. For twenty-seven years thereafter, she lived a life of more abundant significance than ever before. With the wisdom of both life and death, sunshine and sorrow, she helped thousands of people to live with more of victory.

Dr. Goodrich White, former chancellor of Emory University, and his wife, Helen Chappel White, suffered the loss of a splendid son during World War II hostilities. The impact of the loss brought to these two outstanding Christians the whole range of the meaning of faith in the face of death. Mrs. White wrote a stirring book, in which there are some deeply moving passages concerning the significance of life after death. Here is one of these passages:

There is a part of man that triumphantly survives the death of the body and goes on to assume this second more advanced, more permanent phase of living. It is more alive, more vigorous, and interesting than this first phase, for life is of a piece and life is growth. We find a thousand doors opened to us in that life that are closed now and a thousand new experiences in that phase of which we do not now dream.[2]

Mrs. White quotes her distinguished husband in an observation which he made soon after the death of their brilliant son: "You see, I don't believe people die except physically. He's not here, and I miss him more than anybody knows. But I believe he's alive somewhere. I believe I'll see him again. I believe we'll laugh together once more."

The memorial service held in the home church of this fallen hero became a virtual powerhouse of faith, peace, and joy to the people present. Inspired by the departed boy's triumphant spirit, all of the family and so many of his friends turned what might have been a pall of sorrow into songs of triumphant living and fuller serving.

3. *"Prayer—which is the instrument for transforming these resources into strength and comfort"* is a third suggestion listed by Edgar Jackson in his list of resources for handling grief.

"The first thing I did when the doctor came out of the hospital room to tell me that my only child had died," said a splendid Christian man, "was to slip quickly away for a quiet time of prayer—prayer for courage to break the news to my wife, sufficient strength to help her to face the loss, prayer for the willingness to wait to interpret the loss until God should give some perspective not now possible, prayer that from this loss could come a gain of inspiration and strength to many others." Perhaps it is almost unnecessary to report that this man never lost his way in those days of sorrow. Afterward, he and his wife became mother and dad to scores of children with whom they worked as a living memorial to the child they had lost. They brightened many young eyes, cheered many lonely hearts, and sent many lives along to more meaningful living. *Prayer had been a very large factor in their turning their sorrow into a song of love and service.*

Singing at Midnight

Harold W. Ruopp, distinguished minister, lecturer, and author, gave to the world a magnificent message with the title, "Singing at Midnight." Since his truly wonderful discussion explains so beautifully the formula by which many heroes and heroines of this book have turned their sorrows into song, the heart of Dr. Ruopp's message is shared here.

Basing his message on the episode in Acts 16 in which Paul and Silas, chained in prison, at midnight began to pray and to sing praises to God, Dr. Ruopp points out with versatility of discussion and illustration that we, too, in the midnight of our sorrows *can* sing and praise God. He makes three excellent suggestions for handling the midnight of sorrow:

1. *"Accept It."*

Even though the experience is unwanted, unexpected, and extremely bitter, fighting it will only make the experiences more difficult to handle. The wonderful spirit of Job gives

guidance in the matter of accepting grief. Of course, Job
neither wanted nor expected the succession of sorrows
which came to him; yet, even in his hours of greatest loss,
grief, and pain, he cried out with immortal expressions of
faith: "The Lord gave, and the Lord hath taken away;
blessed be the name of the Lord" (Job 1:21). "Though he
slay me, yet will I trust in him" (Job 13:15).

Accepting the grief does not imply welcoming it; rather,
it implies an intelligent recognition that sorrow and loss are
integral parts of life, that the loss in death which has
occurred is beyond human power to alter, that all the self-
blame or condemnation or withdrawal or self-pity or "drug-
ging" of oneself will only delay the inevitable facing up to
the reality of the loss.

*Accepting the grief does not imply ability to explain the
grief.* In fact, Job never did come to the ability to explain
his succession of griefs, and it is possible that an attempt to
explain a grief in the early hours of its arrival may result in
either rash or shallow explanations. Particularly is it important that the individual not conclude that "God sent it, and
I must bow to the will of God." Many losses and griefs are
caused by human negligence or failure or violation of the
laws of the universe established by God. Whatever measures
of chastisement or pruning God initiates are sent *always* for
intelligent and just reasons—helpful reminders, loving
chastisement as instruction, aids to fruitfulness, or as desirable deterrents to greater hurt. A blind assignment of
everything which comes to "the will of God" is a very great
mistake, misinterpreting the justice, goodness, and wisdom
of God, and impairing our own capacity to handle the
experience intelligently.

Dr. Ruopp points out that Katherine Mansfield, aware

that the disease from which she was suffering had only death as its end and days of loneliness, weariness, and depression intervening, wrote these courageous words in her journal: "One must submit. Do not resist. Accept it fully. Make it a part of life." Dr. Ruopp points out that this splendid acceptance of an unwanted experience as a part of life made possible Katherine Mansfield's use of faith and courage and love in transcending the experience. The victory following acceptance made possible her saying shortly before her death: "I feel happy—deep down. All is well."

2. *"Explore It."*

If the individual has accepted sorrow and loss in the spirit described above, he is in position, after the waves of grief have subsided, to explore the reasons, purposes, and possible uses of the experience. Dr. Ruopp suggests these possible questions in the exploration of the sorrow:

What is its nature? What has brought it on? Am I responsible for it? Or is it one of life's inevitables? If I can help it, there is no use worrying about it, for I can set about to change it. If I can't help it, if it is part and parcel of the total life-process, then there is no use worrying about it either, for it lies with a power beyond myself.

I know of many instances in which parents have been faced with heartbreaking actions by their children, including times of suicide. Instead of giving way to self-pity that their children have hurt them so much, they have had the courage to explore the reasons for the actions, not sparing themselves in the search. They haven't screamed accusations at the schools, at "the crowd," at the ingratitude of the children. Instead, they have sat down to a calm, prayer-led search of all possible factors. Whatever there was to be corrected in their own lives for the sake of other children in the family, they corrected. Whatever strength and wisdom they could glean from the experience to share with other people, they did. If, with complete honesty and frankness, they came to the conclusion that they were not at fault in any way, they had the wisdom to stop the frustrating, enervating, and crushing habit of self-blame. The exploration of any experience of grief can be handled wisely in this manner.

3. *"Dedicate It"* is the third suggestion offered by Dr. Ruopp in his stimulating treatise on learning to sing in the midnight of difficulty.

I was overwhelmed by the shared experience of a woman who, with her husband, had suffered a loss which would have tinged the remainder of life with grief for weaker persons. Having no children of their own, she and her husband had adopted a little son. The son had grown in strength of body, mind, and character to the point of being the fulfilment of their highest hope as parents. He was sixteen, full of the happiness of high school, radiant from his first sensations of romance. How glad and proud and grateful were his parents!

One night, as he and high school friends returned from a school event, the fine sixteen-year-old lost his life in a car accident in which the high school students were not at fault. "Killed instantly, no chance for doctors and hospitals to try their hands at healing: our boy is gone," were reactions which could have raced through the minds of the grief-stricken parents. But they were so much wiser than many others in such times of sorrow!

They recognized immediately that the cause of the son's death was human failure; therefore, they did not blame God for the loss. They recognized that, despite their grieving hearts, the boy could not be called back; and that if he had lived, he might have been a broken, inert form for the rest of his life; that life for them must go on, despite the loss of their richest possession, and that they must find ways in which to lose their grief in service to others.

The bereaved mother sought God's guidance to find a way to "lose her grief" in unselfish service—all the more desirable because of the father's protracted absences from home in the fulfilment of his work obligations. In short, *she dedicated her sorrow.*

The guidance came: why not offer her services to the ministers of her little city to perform hospital visitation as a follow-up and complement to the visits of the ministers to their hospitalized church members? Her offer was received with joy; the ministers shared with her daily the calls which she could make to advantage; the hospital staff felt a freedom to call her at any hour of the day or night to come to assist either patients or their distraught families with her magnificent spirit of understanding and love. Not only had she become "an angel of mercy" to so many, but, also, she had "lost" her sorrow in her dedicated ministry to others.

Two personal friends of mine lost their firstborn to a malignancy after a superlative effort of the finest doctors and scientists in America had failed to stop the "killer" in his blood. They turned from the hours of funeral and committal to give themselves with vigor to promoting funds for additional research into blood diseases, hoping thereby to aid the scientists in finding a way to save the children of other parents. *"They dedicated their sorrow too!"*

As a facet of the dedication of their difficulties, sorrows, and losses, many splendid people have followed the example of David and Job. Although David had besought God to spare the life of one of his children and had given evidence of a broken heart, upon the death of the child, this was his reaction:

Then David arose from the earth, and washed, and anointed *himself*, and changed his apparel, and came into the house of the Lord, and worshipped: then he came to his own house; and when he required, they set bread before him, and he did eat. Then said his servants unto him, What thing *is* this that thou hast done? thou didst fast and weep for the child, *while it was* alive; but when the child was dead, thou didst rise and eat bread. And he said, While the child was yet alive, I fasted and wept: for I said, Who can tell *whether* God will be gracious to me, that the child may live? But now he is dead, wherefore should I fast? can I bring him back again? I shall go to him, but he shall not return to me" (2 Sam. 12:20-23).

When the various messengers came in quick succession to tell Job of the losses of his livestock, servants, and children, Job received these shocking reports with this reaction:

Then Job arose, and rent his mantle, and shaved his head, and fell down upon the ground, and worshipped. And said, Naked came I out of my mother's womb, and naked shall I return thither; the Lord gave, and the Lord hath taken away; blessed be the name of the Lord. In all this Job sinned not, nor charged God foolishly (Job 1:20-22).

Surrendering and Serenading

Dr. Ruopp pointed out in the conclusion of his excellent treatise the significance of the concluding words of Acts 16:25, ". . . *and the prisoners heard them.*" Those who were in the same condition of tragedy in which Paul and Silas were, heard their singing at midnight and must have taken courage that others, as badly hurt as they, could sing in the midst of their woes. In short, with their triumphant handling of their sorrows, Paul and Silas "serenaded" others.

A lovely woman had lost her widely-loved husband in death. She and two children faced the future without a breadwinner in the family. Her triumphant faith was explained in this way to many friends who enquired of her "unafraid spirit" as she faced the future: "I believe with all my heart the promise of Deuteronomy 31:8, that God has gone before my children and me to work out ways in which our needs can be met. And if a wonderful God, who knew all the time that my husband would not survive, is out there in the future working in my behalf, it would be more than foolish for me to worry." She serenaded many anxious hearts with her "song at midnight."

A husband and wife who were active participants in several phases of the life of their church, but particularly useful in the adult choir, had lost their only child after months of undulating hope. The whole church had hoped and prayed that medical science could save this only child of this wonderful couple; and the whole church grieved when, on a Friday afternoon, the child was committed to its grave. Everyone normally expected that the exhausted and distraught parents would take time out from church activity —perhaps, going on a trip to "get away from it all."

On Sunday morning, less than forty-eight hours after the burial of their most precious earthly possession, the husband and wife were in the choir, singing with the radiance of a very deep faith, singing in their midnight of sorrow! Regardless of what the listeners heard of the pastor's sermon that morning, they went away with a lesson which must have shamed some and strengthened many: *The Christian's sorrow does not have to become a handicap!*

But Your Sorrow Is Different?

Not really! Its details may be different, but the principles are the same. Its tragedy seems greater to you because it happened to *you*. But even if your sorrow is different or greater, that only means that you have an even better chance to prove the adequacy of God's love, wisdom, presence, and power; for *nothing* that ever befalls a child of God is beyond God's capacity to turn to victory.

And have you remembered that, just as exquisite violin music cannot be played until the violin strings are stretched to the breaking point, it could be that the sweetest and finest music of your life will come if you will lift the strings of your heart—stretched to the breaking point by your sorrow—up to the bow of God's promises and power, and let him play out of your life a rhapsody of triumph over tragedy?

Have you remembered, too, that genuine rose perfume comes only when the rose petals have been crushed to the point that they "give up themselves" in order that the incomparable fragrance of rose perfume may be made available to cheer the lives of many people? From your crushed heart, yielded to the transforming guidance and power of God, fragrance can issue which will turn the bitterness of many other "prisoners" in the prison house of grief into song.

NOTES

1. Luther Robinson, *op. cit.*, p. 78.

2. Helen Chappel White, *With Wings As Angels* (New York: Holt, Rinehart, & Winston, 1953), p. 176.

3. From the book, *One Life Isn't Enough* (St. Paul, Minnesota: Macster Park Publishing Company, 1965). The outline and summary used here are by gracious permission of Dr. Ruopp's widow and of the publishers.

Hello, Old Age!
9 VITALITY OR VEGETATION?

"This is the age of the aged," announced
magazine article, and the writer had good reason for h
title. Whereas, a century ago people were thought to be o
if they were fifty or older, today a person of that age is on
"middle-aged." Whereas the average span of life in 1900 w
forty-nine years, it has come in 1966 to be seventy years.
our nation today, there are already 18,000,000 citizens wl
are sixty-five years of age or older, and it is estimated th
the total will rise to 22,000,000 by 1970. A statistician h
revealed that the total of senior citizens grows by 800 ea
day.

Our God is not only no respecter of *persons:* he is
respecter of *age brackets!* He loves and uses and honors t
aged as notably as he uses the young. Whereas recent c
cades often have reverberated to the chant, "This is the a
of youth," the longer look of the centuries reveals that G
has used people of even advanced years to accomplish so

f his most remarkable purposes. Abraham would have been ssigned by some people to the advanced senior citizens roup in our day; and Moses, with his eighty years at the me of his being chosen to lead the children of Israel out of gypt, would probably not have been mentioned in the hoose-a-leader committee of our time; yet, God used both f them for ventures which would have tested the vigor of venty-year-olds.

A columnist reported an estimate that 64 percent of the orld's great achievements have been done by people who ad passed their sixtieth birthdays. History reveals that erdi completed his well-known opera, *Falstaff*, when he as eighty years of age. Goethe completed his immortal *aust* when he was eighty-three, and a Greek dramatist ompleted his two best known dramas at the age of seventy-ve and eighty-nine.

Have you been brainwashed into "throwing in the sponge" ecause of your age? Have you become a Methuselah, mere- growing older, or a Moses, continuing to be active and seful while growing older? This chapter has grand good ews for you! In essence, the news is this: *even though you ay have retired from the activity in which you earned your velihood for decades or, as a housewife, from the time- and nergy-consuming responsibilities which formerly required ll your time, the possibilities of usefulness, happiness, and ontribution still available to your life are limitless.*

A galaxy of adult friends your age and older have proved nat an intelligent adult is never too old to learn, to grow, to ontribute—and, in some instances, even to earn in chal- nging new activities. They haven't wailed and railed at the orld for not "giving them a place": they have "made a lace" for themselves. Let's meet some of them.

They Retired, but They Didn't Vegetate

An eighty-three-year-old teacher, who retired from publ
school teaching at seventy-three, but who continues to teac
on a part-time basis in nearby college night school, is th
authority for the advice, "If you must retire, don't vegetat
Keep active!" Readers will be inclined to accept his advi
as valid in the light of his sixty-three years of teaching, h
walking now three miles three nights a week to do his teac
ing, his working out frequently and vigorously in a gyr
nasium, and his continuing participation in alumni activiti
and community interests. He has found age no handica

Long before the eighty-three-year-oldster gave out his e
cellent advice, there were many others who were demo
strating in their years of retirement what can be done
keep life vital, growing, accomplishing. As one views the
different lives and varying activities, several observatio
emerge.

1. *Many have continued as much as possible, as long
possible the activities of their preretirement years.* Some ha
been able to continue with full or lessened activity in the
usual work.

Our papers reported to us a few years ago that a Ne
England woman of eighty-six years of age was continui
her work as a sculptor, a work which she had done for six
years. Mrs. Huntington had already done a large number
widely acclaimed equestrian statues, and was busy on h
eighty-sixth birthday with sculpting to complete another f
a Southern university. When asked about her future wor
she replied: "Oh, there are many ideas I'd like to try. Sculp
ing's too much fun, and if I stopped working, people mig
think I'm getting old."

Many doctors have continued in vital practice well beyond
ie normal retirement years. Other professional people and
idependently employed individuals have simply "tipped
ieir hats" to age sixty-five and have continued unabated in
ieir work-time activities. Some who have been obliged to
tire because of institutional requirements—college teachers,
r instance—have offered their services to smaller institu-
ons as visiting staff members or as interim personnel. An
ventor was reported "going strong" at ninety-one years of
çe at his lifetime job of inventing. All of these agree that
an individual's work-time connection makes continuing
tivity in his chosen field possible, he will be wise to con-
nue for as long as wisdom dictates.

Many senior citizens have continued not only their work,
it, also, their LEARNING. In so doing they have heeded the
lvice of a centenarian in the West who, upon being asked
ow he had continued to be useful, youthful, and vital in
s community, replied, "I have taken care to keep growing
me 'new wood' each year." In amplifying his statement,
 said that he had kept on in reading widely, in making
w friends and learning new insights from them, and in
veloping his religious faith to make sure that he kept
arning more about God and about his own relationship to
s fellowman.

A ninety-six-year-old woman seemed surprised that people
ere surprised that she had continued attending seminars
 a college in the East. "After all," she said, "when life
ases to be learning, it ceases to be living." A man of
venty-five, in giving the secret of his vital interest in a
ar-encyclopedic range of knowledge, indicated that he
d never ceased to read and read and read. "Circumstances
 my life have not permitted me to travel widely; there-

fore, on the pages of books which I read, I visit places, meet
people, and learn so much I have not had opportunity to
learn otherwise."

Other retirees in good physical stamina and with money
which the thrift of working years saved up have continued
their learning through travel, and have often amazed their
younger travel companions with their eagerness to learn
Still others have broken the usual pattern of advancing age
by spending much leisure time in meeting new people and
in making new friendships, from which they have learned
in conversation so much that they had hungered to learn
through the years.

Other splendid people have kept on working essentially in
their life callings, but with different approaches or applica
tions, often with reduced compensation, sometimes with no
pay at all. *Parade Magazine* presented a splendid vignette of
a man and wife couple who, upon retirement, were accepted
by the Peace Corps and became two of the 154 people in the
Corps at that time who were over fifty years of age—a group
including a sixty-nine-year-old mechanic, a seventy-six-year
old water supply engineer, and a group of sixty-five-year-old
teachers.[1]

News comes of the retirement of an eighty-two-year-old
adjutant general of a state national guard, who earlier had
"tailored down" his military activities from a national scope
to a state assignment. There was news, also, of a senior
citizen who, at eighty-six years of age, was tilling a large
garden from a wheelchair, since he could no longer super
vise his ranch aboard his thirty-two-year-old horse! Many
were inspired by a *Reader's Digest* condensation of a book
concerning Maurice Lee, who at seventy-seven years of age
had become a vital advocate and personal example of using

ne's working years' talents in constructive activities during
tirement years. By precept and example he has pointed
it convincingly that there *are* many and wonderful ways
 which a retiree can put his resources of working years to
nstructive use for the joy of his own life and for the benefit
 society.[2]

A CONTINUING OF HOBBIES into the retirement years has
een a source of stimulating joy to many retired people. I
ve ridden a golf cart around a course with an eighty-two-
ar-old man who plays virtually every weekday on which
e weather permits. In addition to keeping his mind and
dy agile, the hobby has been a grand investment of time,
 which he has an abundance; and, in keeping apace of the
lf world and in meeting delightful new friends, he feels in
od touch with his day. A seventy-two-year-old man of my
rsonal knowledge dons his track uniform and takes a two
ile trot daily, just as he has done through all of his working
ars. A lovely woman of postretirement age continues
idly her hobby of piano music. Another, who has never
fered a picture for sale, continues to paint with delight.
ill another takes great joy in following the weekly food
ges for stimulating new recipes, with which she delights
r neighbors and friends. A fourth woman, who is in her
ghties, still has the prettiest yard and gardens in her
ock.

CONTINUING SERVICE ACTIVITIES have kept so many retired
ople happy and useful. Beloved "Miss Lena" in my city
es not let her ninety-three years serve as an excuse to stop
aching her cherished class of women in her church. Hun-
eds of civic clubs have as their most active and useful
embers retired people who, with more time now available,
ve become even more useful in between-meeting activities

sponsored by their clubs. Thousands of retired ministers have become "heaven-sent blessings" as supply preachers and interim pastors. Who knows how many thousands of women of retirement age, arms now emptied of their own children and grandchildren, are angels of mercy in continuing, so often without compensation, in churches and for friends the activity for which they have both love and skill—the giving of tender, loving care to little ones. These have derived an emotional satisfaction completely essential to happiness at any age: *the joy of being needed and wanted!*

2. *Many retired people have resumed enriching activities which were interrupted in earlier years, finding in the resumption new gratifications and usefulness.*

Some "oldsters" have resumed education of formal nature by returning to school and even by obtaining degrees. To their delight, they have found that the "youngsters" not only do not resent their presence on the campus and in the classes but have received them in cordial spirit. One man, highly successful in business through the years, entered college as a freshman following his retirement from his career. In his final year (in his sixties) he was top man in his class in scholarship and was elected president of Phi Beta Kappa by the students of that academic honor group, most of them young enough to be his grandchildren!

As these pages are being prepared, the newspapers have carried reports of a seventy-nine-year-old man who returned to university for completion of a program which was interrupted in 1909, and of a woman in her eighties whose college life was interrupted in 1911. She doesn't intend to join the "rocking chair brigade" upon the completion of her degree; despite her being an octogenarian, she plans to travel around the world. The seventy-nine-year-old "Joe College" reports that he came back to university because he believes in higher education and just wanted to complete that part of his life.

Even more courageous, doubtless, are the retired men and women who have returned to complete high school work. A retired couple feared that their association with teen-agers would not be welcomed by the teeners; but, to their surprise and delight, the high school group accepted them in a complimentary sense, sharing the feeling that "the two of you can help us to see the relation of what we are studying now to the real problems which you faced through your years of living." A Virginia school custodian, retiring at sixty-eight, returned to night school to complete an education which was interrupted when he was in the third grade so many years before!

With high schools, junior and senior colleges, night schools, opportunity schools, trade and vocational schools multiplying and within reach of practically every retired person in our nation, many other adults beyond sixty are experiencing the thrill of completing educational programs which were interrupted decades ago. Still others are attending opportunity schools on a noncredit basis, simply to increase their joy through increased knowledge.

The resumption of interrupted activities includes, too, a taking up again of hobbies and skills which many adults had dropped in their busy years. Painting, sewing, carpentry, mechanics, golf, music, writing, stenography, and gardening demonstrate the wide range of resumed hobbies and skills reported by a survey of retired people.

One of the most useful areas of resumed activity in the lives of people beyond sixty-five is the area of church activity. So many adults who had maintained a regular connection with their churches, but whose work-time activities either prevented their offering as much of their time in service pursuits as their abilities justified, or who rationalized themselves out of adequate participation in their churches, have found tremendous need for their talents and vast joy for themselves in unselfish service. A South Carolina physician is typical of this group: since his sixty-fifth birthday he has been an active deacon, Bible teacher, Sunday School superintendent, superintendent of leadership training, and a participant in music and fellowship activities of his church. A church bulletin of 1965 announced that he had received his four-hundredth Church Study Course award in his seventy-fifth year and that he had proved in a convincing and wonderful way that life can really begin at sixty-five!

3. *An inspiring group of retirees have "kept on living abundantly"* by entering new doors of activity and usefulness. These have illustrated the statement of a contemporary writer: "A new purpose . . . a new interest and activity help a person build a new image so necessary for most." [3]

Doubtless, the most noted example of an older person's entering new doors of activity is that of Grandma Moses. She had gone to work at twelve years of age as a hired girl, had married a farmer at twenty-seven, had mothered ten children, had continued farm work until she was in her late seventies. When her doctor ordered to give up her farm work, the only work she had ever known, she did not take to the wailing wall or to the bench of idleness. Instead, she took up painting when she was nearly eighty; and, without instruction other than the instinct of her mind and the prompting of her heart, she painted what admiring critics called "the best primitive art, the best of 'folk tradition' in painting, the finest contribution to our recovery of the primitive freshness of the American scene." At the time of her death at one hundred and one years of age, her work had appeared on 100-million Christmas cards and in innumerable other media. *For those retirees who decry their limited education, hard lives, restricted travel, and no special training, Grandma Moses will stand forever as a refutation of their feelings that "it's too late, and I'm too old to start anything new now" feelings.*

But Grandma Moses is not alone in the inspiration which the life of a senior citizen can give. A distinguished minister, retired because of age and limited strength, began a new ministry of tremendous significance—a ministry of intercessory prayer in behalf of people who write to him concerning problems of their lives. A charming woman, retired by age from her work and by illness to her bed, offered her services to her church to organize a mailing list of the church membership on the basis of birthdays and to mail out birthday greetings as the birthdays came. She has become the "Sunshine Lady" of that congregation. When a local newspaper reporter interviewed this lovely one, she ignored both her age and infirmity and said with radiant confidence, "I have so much to live for!"

A retired couple decided to "tithe their waking hours," 8 A.M. to 10 P.M., giving the resultant hour-and-a-half to visiting people who needed visitors, to writing notes of consolation and cheer, to assisting neighbors who were ill, and to doing whatever else they were needed to do. They reported in a column which is designed for senior citizens that the "tithe" of their time had already moved up to three hours a day, and that their joy had increased tremendously.[4]

Another large group of retired people have entered new doors by taking up skills and hobbies which the busy working years had not permitted. A retired businessman, who had been impressed by the speed and skill of his stenographers through the years, began the study of shorthand and typewriting. Another man who had had a desire through all of his busy years to learn a foreign language achieved a remarkable command of the Spanish language. Still another man, yearning through the years to find fulfilment in writing, found that his retirement writings were good enough to be welcomed by the newspapers in his area. And a seventy-one-year-old woman who had wanted all of her life to learn to swim wrote to a columnist to ask for an advertised leaflet on the subject, Learn to Swim. The discerning columnist observed: "I'll bet she learns too, and I am sure that she will never grow old."[5]

To demonstrate that there are the daring and adventurous ones in every age bracket, there are those of the retirement years who have made the front pages with their daring adventures. In 1965, a seventy-one-year-old adventurer made a 10,000 mile solo voyage in a sail-powered raft and gave cheer to millions of his fellows of sunset years by having emblazoned on the sail the words, AGE UNLIMITED.

His courage and daring were matched by husband and wife, both in their late sixties, who took a covered wagon trip from East to West. . . . And by the courage of Miles Jones of San Antonio, who at seventy-four years of age began to build ramps for chair-bound people of his city, so that they could wheel themselves out from "imprisonment" in their houses, making no charge for his work or for the materials, daring to believe that the money to build these $40.00-each ramps would come "from somewhere." It did![6]

A host of other retired people in entering new doors of opportunity have found usefulness and fulfilment in work in children's homes, in voluntary service in retirement homes, in hospital services as needed by chaplains and librarians, in church visitation, in telephone ministries of consolation and cheer, in service in Red Cross workrooms, in visiting shut-ins, in visiting or working voluntarily in homes for unwed mothers, in participating in neighborhood discussion groups, in working with organizations which minister to under-privileged children and promote summer camps for them, in arts and crafts, and in organizing or helping in group activities planned by churches and communities for senior citizens.

This last-named activity in the foregoing list has infinite possibilities; and, in hundreds of communities throughout our nation, a potential use of retired people's abilities awaits the initiative of some senior citizen who will stop regarding age as a handicap and who will "wake up and live." In addition to initiating a worthy and comprehensive spiritual ministry to the aged and the aging, these "waked up" senior citizens can make themselves available to the many-faceted needs of their communities, which can use their skills to advantage while giving to these active retirees the incomparable gratification of being productive, creative, and useful.

Have You Learned the Secret?

Are the continued activity and usefulness of so many people into years beyond retirement, their refusing to believe that old age is a handicap, explainable in any one terse way, in some special formula, in some secret of truth they have learned? Better than any other explanation I have read is:

Life is a lively process of *becoming*. If you haven't added to your interests during the past year, if you are thinking the same thoughts, telling the same anecdotes, relating the same personal experiences, having the same predictable reactions—you may as well wake up to the unpleasant truth that, regardless of your age, rigor mortis of the personality has started to set in. Some people seem to have a knack of staying interesting—and interested. They've got a secret! *They simply don't let themselves stop becoming.* They keep themselves mentally and emotionally lithe by getting excited about new things: new activities, new friends, new ideas. They widen their interests in books, art, music, politics, world affairs, current events. They stay alert! Some of the things that absorbed them in the past may seem less important to them than they once did. Their old leaves drop off, but they sprout new ones![7]

Some senior citizen-reader of this chapter, inspired by those who have found the secret to continued growth and usefulness, may reach out with the question, "How can I begin to be a person who keeps *becoming?*" Let's hear the advice of other retirees.

ATTITUDE is stressed as a determinant; and on the basis of its positivism of negativism the retired person will automatically choose between continuation of a full life and the tragic state of vegetation. Feeling that life is, to all achievement purpose, finished, giving way to self-pity, yielding to self-satisfaction over one's past achievements, succumbing to the fear of failure in undertaking new ventures, false pride in unwillingness to learn from other—even younger—people, a "hardening of attitudes" to the degree of resistance to any change of attitude or opinion, the feeling that one who has worked hard to retirement has a right to waste his time if he desires, and a fixation of thought and premium on the past are all attitudes which guarantee the retired person a growing unhappiness and uselessness.

On the other hand, an attitude of positivism, a forward look, a zest for new experiences can make of any older person a youthful soul.

ADJUSTABILITY, the second determinant stressed by many successful senior citizens, will be much more quickly achieved if the right attitude toward advancing years has been developed.

Mrs. Lu Travis tells of the mistaken concept which she and her husband first had toward adjustment to retirement and their coming later to the genuinely sensible adjustment. They laid aside the work which had been their life during the preretirement years and went into a virtual frenzy of travel and other activities—evidently as an escape from admitting that they were retired. Physical factors necessitated their giving up the new pattern of accelerated activity; and, in times of thought, loneliness, and near-despair they came to this realization: both of them needed to continue what had been their life prior to retirement—drawing for him, writing for her—but in ways appropriate to their present ages and in ways which would help other people unselfishly. When they adjusted themselves thus, peace and happiness came to them.

Therefore, Mrs. Travis urges people to continue to be productive but with a relativity to their ages. "If you are an artist, paint as an artist of sixty-five, not as you did thirty years ago," she advises. To the makers of cookies and other pastries she gives the reminder that they continue to dabble in those delicacies, but that they become more practical in their products.

"Be your own precious age and love it," Mrs. Travis reminds others.

Other adjustments suggested by Mrs. Travis are these:

If driving runs up your blood pressure, sell the car and call a taxi. Taxi drivers are fun.

Walking is a fine, old-fashioned way of getting around, bringing acquaintance with your neighbors. . . .

All of life is readjustment. . . . Life is change.[8]

News dispatches in a recent year told of an inventor, long past retirement age but still busy at inventing, who had adjusted through the years from "shed-in-the-backyard" individual inventing to laboratory research, then to vast cooperative undertakings in which several different types of research firms are involved. Small wonder that at an "advanced" age he was still productive and happy!

In addition to attitude and adjustability, many still-growing senior citizens have stressed ACTIVITY CONTINUATION— the keeping alive intellectually, the keeping resilient through activities suitable for their ages; and ADVANCEMENT—the expanding of the scope of interest and friendships in a more relaxed manner than in the busy career days prior to retirement; and, finally, the APPLICATION OF A SENSE OF HUMOR to the changed status of one's life beyond retirement.

A businessman of ninety-two was advised by his doctor that the time had come in which he must slow down somewhat. The newspapers reported the nonagenarian's reply thus: "What? And be hit by a taxicab?" That sense of humor had probably saved him from many difficult circumstances all through the years. A beloved woman of ninety-six, now in a retirement home, is the bright light of the home with her ever-present sense of humor.

My paternal grandmother lived to be old enough to enjoy her great-grandchildren and never ceased to be the life of any group in which she was present. Through a hard life on a stubborn farm, through mothering fourteen children, through wars and financial panics and multiple difficulties she had lived and moved with laughter in her heart and on her lips.

Olive Higgins Prouty, on the occasion of the fiftieth anniversary reunion of her graduating class at Smith College, presented this delightful, humorous bit of wisdom, titled "After Seventy":

> Pamper the body,
> Prod the soul,
> Accept limitations
> But play the role.
> Withdraw from the front
> But stay in the fight,
> Avoid isolation,
> Keep in sight,
> Beware of reminiscing
> (Except to a child),
> To forgetting proper names
> Be reconciled,
> Refrain from loquacity,
> Be crisp and concise—
> And regard self-pity
> As a cardinal vice.

Old Age: Handicap or Happiness?

Every individual senior citizen will determine what the answer to that question will be. Of this we may be sure: old age is *not* being a handicap to many thousands of our senior citizens and does not have to be a handicap to anyone. It is logical to ask now the question inscribed on a Rust Craft greeting card (Used by permission):

How Old Are You?

Age is a quality of mind.
If you have left your dreams behind,
    If hope is lost,
If you no longer look ahead,
    If your ambition's fires are dead,
Then you are old.
But if from life you take the best,
    And if in life you keep the jest,
        If love you hold,
No matter how the years go by,
    No matter how the birthdays fly,
You are not old!

NOTES

1. Ed Keester, "The Peace Corps: One Answer to Useful Old Age
Parade Magazine, August 4, 1963.

2. Allen Rankin, *Harvest Years* (San Francisco: Harvest Years Publishir
Co., January, 1963.)

Harvest Years is a monthly publication for senior citizens. Inquiri
concerning its availability and costs may be sent to Harvest Years Publishir
Company, 681 Marker Street, San Francisco, California.

3. Henry Schmidt, Jr., *Christian Herald*, August, 1965, p. 32.

4. The Golden Years, a column by Thomas Collins, in *Houston* (Texas
Post.

5. "Why Grow Old?" a column by Josephine Lowman, in *Greensbor*
(North Carolina) *Record*, September 22, 1962.

6. "The Quiet People," *Guideposts*, October, 1965, p. 15.

7. "They've Got a Secret," *Guideposts*, September, 1965, p. 15, fro
Whatsoever Things, Gerald Horton Bath, Editor. (Horton).

8. Reprinted by permission of *Christian Life* magazine, Copyright Augus
1965, Christian Life Publications Inc., Gundersen Drive and Schmale Roa
Wheaton, Illinois 60187, pp. 36ff.

Personal Word from
10   the Author

      Induced by an accident shortly after I had entered public school, osteomyelitis retired me from school to a long period of hospitalization, surgery, and confinement to bed. In my childhood this particular type of bone trouble was difficult to control; and the frightening possibility that, controlled in one area, it would break out in another, kept doctors, family, and friends in years of apprehension.

By the time of my twelfth birthday two facts emerged: the bone trouble had been cured, but I would be permanently lame with a dwarfed and weakened left limb, at that time four inches shorter than the right one. First, crutches and, later, a raised shoe and walking cane became my permanent aids to walking. "What a shame that he will always be a cripple," were the words which, though whispered by well-meaning friends, fell upon my ears often in childhood.

Even then I could not feel that physical lameness *had* to make a hurtful difference in an individual's life; and now I rejoice to declare, with the experience of these many years to sustain my conviction, that, far from being a "dampening" or deterring factor, physical lameness has been one of life's richest gifts to me.

During long hospital experiences I met magnificent people who enriched my life immeasurably. During long confinement I learned to love good reading, grammar, and word study. Of necessity I learned early the significance of prayer and the wisdom and power of God's Word. From the fellowship of suffering I developed a deep desire to help to alleviate sufferings which problems of any kind so often bring into people's lives.

In short, physical lameness has brought to me rich resources of strength which, otherwise, I might have failed to possess. It has brought to me, as only personal suffering can, an understanding of other people who suffer in body, mind, or spirit; and with that understanding has come a warm desire to help. For me, physical lameness has opened windows, unlocked doors, widened horizons, deepened understandings, heightened sympathies, sharpened powers, and enriched with spiritual victories. Thank God for lameness!

Detour Became Blessing

It was mid-afternoon of June 22, 1947. There was a terrific automobile collision in which the fine young man who was driving me was completely blameless. Though my driver was only slightly injured, I was much undone with terrific fractures in my already lame left hip and leg. Through my mind in those moments of excruciating pain

here raced the stark prospect of losing the left leg; for, at
that moment, I felt that amputation would be merciful.

So, into a hospital and into an intricate traction bed I was
put. Mysterious whispered uncertainties and ten weeks in
traction before a cast could be applied did bring wonder-
ings into my mind concerning the future. In the midst of
the days of uncertainty there came to me a telegram from
friends, concluding with the promise of Isaiah 40:31, "But
they that wait upon the Lord shall renew their strength;
they shall mount up with wings as eagles; they shall run,
and not be weary; and they shall walk, and not faint." Like
rain upon parched earth there settled into my heart the assurance that this experience, too, would become a source of
strength and a rich blessing.

Thanks to the skill of a magnificent young surgeon, I
came through that experience in much better physical condition than before the accident. He had so skilfully attended
to the injured hip and limb that the limb is now straighter
than at any time since my childhood, and the left leg is one
inch longer than before the accident! I can now walk with
much more of efficiency and comfort . . . and those eight
months abed proved to be the richest time of spiritual
strengthening I have had since college days.

Disappointment—His-appointment

Though they are too deeply personal to discuss in this
little chapter, there have come to me in my post-college
years three times of keen, almost bitter disappointment. In
each of the three instances there was a combination of
denial, frustration, and unmistakable loss of what I had
hoped for. I would be unrealistic, if not actually dishonest,
to say that I accepted the disappointments with "smiling

resignation," for there were such keen heartaches in all three instances that both smile and joy were temporarily missing from my heart.

Having learned, however, the magnificent truth of Romans 8:28 and 37, Isaiah 41:10 and 13, and Philippians 4:13 and 19, I did commit each of those disappointments to God's will and to his wisdom and power. As in many, many instances in life, the proof that my disappointments were "blessings in disguise" did not come immediately. There are instances in which only the slow perspective of the years can reveal God's better way.

Now, however, I am able to affirm with conviction and joy that in all three of those instances, my disappointments were really His-appointments; for, in each of those matters, much more of good has come to me, and through me much more of good has come to other people, because God "rearranged" my plans and hopes for better plans and wiser hopes. I thank God so often now for his wise ministry through what had appeared to be frustrating disappointments.

Outside the incomparable assurances in which the Bible abounds, there is no passage which cheers and strengthens me more than the immortal John Greenleaf Whittier poem, "The Eternal Goodness," a part of which is quoted here.

> I know not what the future hath
>   Of marvel or surprise,
> Assured alone that life and death
>   His mercy underlies.
>
> I know not where His islands lift
>   Their fronded palms in air;
> I only know I cannot drift
>   Beyond His love and care.

The Parade Continues:

11 HEROES KEEP COMING!

Through the pages of our book have marched so many conquerors of the high hurdles of handicaps—from the past, and from the busy world of today. But the parade continues with new joiners-in-its-ranks daily, challenging inspirations to our day!

For instance, at this writing the most recent Hurdle Awards Banquet in Dallas recognized as its top honoree Albert L. Baker, a twenty-seven-year-old quadruplegic, who, despite his severe physical impairments, has achieved such a high level of performance through an IBM Programing Course, that he is employed by a large corporation and competes quite successfully with nondisabled personnel. He maintains his own apartment, provides his own transportation, cares for all of his personal needs, and has become independent physically and economically.

Given honorable mention in the same banquet were eight others. *Audley Blackburn, Jr.,* blind since birth, is a success-

ful college student and headed for theological seminary. . . .
Miss Lynda Carol Bryant, victim of cerebral palsy with
considerable involvement, has achieved both bachelor's and
master's degrees from outstanding universities, and is planning to be a speech therapist. . . . *Miss Carol Cunningham,*
victim of a rare bone condition which results in numerous
fractures and deformities, teaches English, having won her
university degree in that subject. . . . *Mrs. Mary Ann Davis,*
polio-smitten since age twelve, graduated from university
and took a postgraduate course in medical technology, and
works now as a medical technologist—in addition to maintaining her home and driving a car. . . .

Armando Delgado, handicapped by the loss of both legs
in an accident is studying horology, serving an apprentice-
ship in a jewelry store, and demonstrating great courage in
overcoming his handicap. . . . *Ward Jameson* was seventeen
at the time of recognition, a cerebral palsy patient, but leading a life of challenge and normalcy: dating regularly, driving his own car, participating actively in student activities
despite a speech impairment and movements that are tedious
and difficult. . . . *Miss Eileen Rogers,* crippled by cerebral
palsy and deaf, detoured by much hospitalization and
surgery, has become expert in lipreading and is a highly
prized typist for a great business concern. . . . *Mrs. Jo Walker,*
handicapped by muscular dystrophy since childhood, and
in a wheelchair since she was eleven years of age, did not
permit her handicap to keep her from high school graduation and the heroic living of a well-balanced life: happy
marriage, splendid daughter, successful secretarial work, and
participation in several church and youth group activities.

To this star-studded list of conquerors of handicaps in a
single city can be added the inspiring experiences of many

throughout our land. Our newspapers have thrilled us in recent months with stories and pictures of several young people who have demonstrated the neither-down-nor-out spirit: *a fifteen-year-old girl,* born without hands, but skilful in her use of artificial limbs—so much so, that she is a "B" student. . . . *An Oklahoma lad,* born with only partial hands, but so skilful in baseball that he became an inspiration to a whole city. . . . *A young woman in the East,* injured to the point of losing her hands in an accident, but who adjusted wonderfully to artificial hands and became excellent in painting. . . . And the *thirteen-year-old Michigan junior high boy* who plays all sports despite the loss of a leg—playing touch football, soccer, and baseball on crutches, and playing basketball without crutches, hopping up and down the court, becoming a leading scorer!

Demonstrating the reliance of spirit which can turn a handicapped person's interests and skills to areas not before contemplated are *Michael Crummel,* who lost his right leg and half of his left foot in an accident when he was six years of age, but who is developing remarkable ability in art, stimulating interest in car replicas, and growth of plant and animal life . . . and *Bobby Green,* dauntless Texas high school student who lost a leg as a result of an accident and could no longer march with the high school band, whose fancy marching and drilling had become a prized activity of his life, but who plays in the "sitting band," announces the marches, and makes introductions at athletic contests. Bobby's father, knowing of my keen interest in Bobby's recovery and readjustment, added this delightful paragraph to a recent letter: "One thing led to another, and he now has his disc jockey license and does spot announcing at a radio station. He is in an unusual position in that almost

every young person has his eyes on him. . . . I have told him
that he may be able to have more influence on young people
in these few years than I have or will have in a lifetime."

Adults Too!

But the youngsters are by no means the only heroes of
the contemporary section of the parade of the handicapped;
for, indeed, the adults are there in number and inspiration
too. *Mrs. Pauline Gorson,* for instance, who was smitten with
polio many years ago just one semester short of high school
graduation, but who returned to school and received her
high school diploma at fifty-four years of age despite the
added handicap of blindness, gives cheer to thousands who
take her example as an assurance of their ability to overcome. . . . And the *violinist* who lost all four fingers of the
hand with which he manipulated the strings of the violin,
but who has learned to use the thumb of that hand so skilfully on the strings that he is able to continue his violin
playing, tells through his smile and amazingly good performance that even apparent catastrophies are not insur-
mountable, . . . and *Mrs. Draughon,* North Carolina's outstanding handicapped person for the current year, though
chair-bound from a permanently impaired back, has become
both beloved and self-supporting through great skill in
pastries.

Not only golf devotees, but people of all sports were
thrilled to read the May, 1966, report of the courageous decision of a blind piano tuner to take up golf for a recreation.
Of him, a sportswriter Tom Ensign, in the *Hollywood* (Florida) *Sun-Tattler,* said: "Everett Proctor is living proof that
no matter how severe a handicap is, it can be overcome. All
it takes is an abundance of courage and cat-like patience."

And in the same week there was announcement of the Southern States Amputee Golf Tournament!

Even the men and women of the "Golden Years" category are delightfully evident in the contemporary section of the parade of the victorious. *Miss Layona Green* of Georgia celebrated her hundredth birthday with a "rendezvous with the mighty" in Washington, D.C., prior to leaving by plane for Brazil, where she had spent almost forty years in mission work, coming later back to Georgia for a busy life in church work and journalism. . . . The inimitable *Casey Stengel*, retired from managing a baseball team at nearly seventy-five years of age (only because of a broken hip!) walked straight into Baseball's Hall of Fame in March of 1966 by unanimous vote of the Veterans Committee. . . . *Lee Meriwether* returned from his seventy-ninth trip abroad shortly before his hundred and third birthday. . . . A *distinguished pianist* gave concerts at eighty-one years of age to a standing-room-only audience in New York and other cities and was accorded an ovation. . . . An *outstanding violinist,* in his late seventies, was acclaimed for his concert and for the never ebbing youthfulness of his spirit. . . . And a recent news headline announces that the incomparable Walt Disney at age sixty-four looks only to the future in stimulating plans for what most people regard as "post-active" years!

A Queen, Indeed!

Embodying the whole drama of victory over handicaps as magnificently as anyone of contemporary life has done—and, indeed, as well as any of the distinguished victors of the past have done—is the charming, radiant, inspiring Miss Handicapped America of 1965, *Miss Lida Shoemaker of Colorado.*

Polio "came to stay" when Miss Shoemaker was only nine

years of age, leaving as permanent indications of its presence an almost total loss of use of lower limbs. After protracted therapy and training in the use of braces and canes,
she completed all of the public school curriculum in regular
school attendance. Upon entering college, she discovered
that she could manage her getting about more easily in a
wheelchair, because her back and arm muscles were strong
enough to manipulate the chair to a nearly maximum capacity. She is now able to "manage" or "jump" a six-inch
curb in her chair, to fold the chair, get into her car, and to
drive with ease!

College was challenging and enjoyable for her, and she
came through with a bachelor of music education degree.
Since graduation from college, she has taught in both Iowa
and Colorado, and in the summer of 1965 she became the
"Miss Handicapped America" for the twelve-month period
ahead.

Her philosophy, too, is typical of the wholesome "wisdom
of soul" which has piloted so many people to heartwarming
victory over handicaps. Let's hear her own words, given in
a letter to me: "We all have handicaps of some sort; but
upon self-acceptance the handicap can become greatly mini-
mized and at times used to benefit. . . . The casual acceptance of my handicap by my students and friends is due
largely, I believe, to my own casual acceptance."

We salute you, Miss Handicapped America, as queen of
the handicapped, and as queen, too, of the hearts of multiple
millions who view the contemporary section of the parade
of the neither-down-nor-out brigade. You and the domain
over which you exercise symbolic queenship have moved
many people to admiration of vast dimensions and to resolution that, should they be called to join the parade, they will

try to march with the secret of victory which has made you and your subjects so wonderful.

L'Envoi

And, so, into tomorrow the parade of the "Wouldn't Give Up" soldiers marches. Some who read these lines, now in the peak of health and fitness, may find themselves thrust into that march with the suddenness of the breaking of a bough in a windstorm. A day which dawns in the splendor of perfection may leave some reader with a come-to-stay imperfection. It is my hope that inspiration from these episodes of victory-despite-handicaps, seen in the wonderful ones who have marched through the pages of this book, will be stored away in each reader's heart as fuel with which to light a fire of faith if he or she should be called upon to join this parade of heroes and heroines.

Walk and talk with the victors in this book again in reviewing their lives; appropriate their secrets of victory even before you need those secrets. Then nothing which the future may bring will find you unprepared. To the symphonic accompaniment of faith, courage, and perseverance, you, too, can sing with joy and confidence, "I can do all things through Christ which strengtheneth me."

ACKNOWLEDGMENTS

There may be writers who need no help outside their brilliant minds and resourceful spirits, and who can write books with little or no assistance. The author of this book is not in that echelon of magicians; for, without the wonderful help which he receives from others, he would be either book-less or an author whose books would have much less in them!

Although much help has come from sources which are the general heritage and possession of all of us, there have been helpers of whose assistance I am keenly aware and for which I am deeply grateful. First, there have been those who have assisted in sharing inspiring information concerning people who have overcome handicaps.

Some of these helpful friends are these: Dr. Howard Aultman, Dr. Donald Bell, Dr. and Mrs. Wade Bryant, Miss Eleanor Ray Burns, Mr. Clark Chesnut, Mrs. Charles Davis, Miss Lorene Farmer, First Baptist Church of Marietta (Georgia), Gardner-Webb College Public Relations, Mr. Paul Green, Rev. John Harris, Dr. and Mrs. James Landes, Mr. Frank Logan, Dr. and Mrs. Roy McGlamery, Mrs. Charles Martin, Dr. Hope Owen, Mrs. Mae H. Owens, Dr. Eugene Patterson, Dr. William Hall Preston, Mrs. Agnes Pylant, Miss Faye Ross (all information concerning the Hurdle Awards), Dr. Paul Staake, Dr. Joseph Stiles, Mrs. James H. Street, Press Services: Associated Press, United Press-International. . . . and YOU whose sharings the limitations of one book precluded.

Second, there are those who have facilitated the preparation of the manuscripts through making possible the secre-

159

tarial help so necessary to initial and completed drafts. These wonderful friends are Mr. and Mrs. Frank Fair, Mr. and Mrs. Hudson Titmus, Mr. Jimmy Karam, Dr. William Smith, and Mr. John C. Brown. To these beloved friends, the author is almost inexpressably grateful.

Third, to Mr. Alvin Davis and his superb staff at beautiful Callaway Gardens in Georgia the author is highly grateful.

Fourth, to friends of the "Fraternity of the Handicapped" who have helped in the preparation of this book, I am grateful in a particularly keen sense of fellowship. Miss Jane Merchant composed the title poem, Mrs. Elsie Mangum Gunter prepared the design for the front jacket, Miss Nellie Faye Parker prepared the original designs from which the chapter introductory drawings are taken, and Miss Wynelle Ray did the typewriting for one of the final drafts of the manuscript.

Fifth, to my Intern-Associate, Jerry Merriman, I am indebted and sincerely grateful; for, in the long-time preparation of this book he helped significantly in the gathering and processing of materials, spending long hours of toil at the typewriter in assisting the author. Without his valuable help, this book's appearance would have been delayed greatly.

Sixth, to Miss Dorothy Pulley I feel most grateful for indispensable aid of highest quality in the final handling of the manuscript before it went to the publishers. For her skill and for her keen sense of interest in the mission of the book, I am abidingly grateful.

Finally, to all who read these pages and find help in them, and who share the help found herein with any others who need inspiration to try again, I am indebted and abundantly grateful.